The
LOW
Cholesterol
GLUTTON

D0806900

The
LOW
Cholesterol
GLUTTON

Sonia Allison

Absolute Press

Absolute Press, 14 Widcombe Crescent, Bath, England
© Sonia Allison 1990
© (Illustrations) Katherine Greenwood 1990

First printed October 1990
Reprinted November 1990
Reprinted November 1991
Reprinted January 1994

Cover and book design: Monica Chia

Front cover photography: Paul Dunn

Photoset and printed by The Longdunn Press Ltd, Bristol

ISBN 0 948230 33 9

DEDICATION

To wildlife artist Roy Chaffin and his wife Dinah
for reasons only they will understand.

GRATITUDE TO

Jon Croft of Absolute Press for taking the book on board and Nicki Morris for being such a super editor and friend into the bargain.

Don Steele of the Family Heart Association for support and co-operation and Annette Zakary, the Association's Dietician/Counsellor, for checking out my facts with humour, patience and tact.

All my guinea pigs. My husband as ever and our dear and close friends for eating their way through innumerable experiments and providing constructive criticism with never a word of complaint. Our kind and good neighbours for doing the same and Maureen upstairs for putting up with unaccustomed smells for months on end and ringing down to see if we were ablaze and about to expire when I was cooking Tandoori chicken – yet again!

Dr England and his dedicated team at Watford General Hospital's haematology department for looking after me so conscientiously for nearly a decade. And for encouraging me to write this book.

Our own GP's, Dr John May and Dr Edward Rieu, for their help, kindness and care and for treating me as if I were a real live human being despite my idiosyncrasies. Likewise the reception and nursing staff at our local health centre.

The Thalasso Club (Helianthal) at St Jean de Luz for helpful information and ideas.

Flax Foods in Bushey Heath, Hertfordshire, for supplying me with the pick of smoked salmon and salmon trimmings for some of the recipes.

Hitchcock's fish stall at Watford market for the best fish ever.

The following for donating products to the cause:

Royal Greenland Smoked Halibut Napolina tomato and oil products
California raisins Dolmio pasta Lea and Perrins Candia olive oil from
Crete Meridian Foods Mazola Tabasco Billington's sugar Brittany
Prince artichokes Conservation Grade Meat (The Pure Meat Company)
from Asda Brother Microwave Ovens Swan Housewares
Cauldron Foods (Tofu) Pelham Venison Company

CONTENTS

INTRODUCTION

How's this for a proposition? Eat your way to healthier life without forfeiting all the treats, luxuries and goodies you thought, shock-horror, were a thing of the past when your doctor declared, "Your cholesterol is too high. Go on a diet", handing you some cheerful-looking leaflets put out by chemical companies and the food industry. What he didn't tell you was how dreary the regime was going to be, how dull, how uninspired, how frustrating. But you soon found out, didn't you, as you suffered a daily dose of chicken or fish, or the other way round, enlivened with the occasional plate of baked beans on toast, a microwaved jacket potato with what my husband calls scrape ("safe" margarine) and, when you were feeling self-indulgent and not too worried about the waistline, a meringue with a scoop of sorbet. All blameless stuff.

What I want you to do now for a minute or two is forget boredom and look on the brighter side of the cholesterol culinary coin. There is one, I promise you, so you can forget all about martyrdom and self-pity and start to enjoy eating again, look forward to meals with pleasure and, literally, gorge to your heart's content. That should lift the spirits for starters.

Tell me, does my grandmother's Fragrant Bread Pudding, updated with Brandied Mango Sauce, sound like deprivation? Or Courgette and Broccoli Soup, or sliced Kipper Fillets Marinated in Lemon Juice with slender onion

rings. No, of course they don't. Do Smoked Salmon Strips sautéed with sesame seeds and served with hot pumpkin cubes sound self-sacrificial? Or Chilli con Pollo with brown and wild rice. Or Ginger Pudding with Apple Sauce. No, of course they don't.

Ethnic and closer-to-home creations are all there for you to savour whether you are a vegetarian with a penchant for Spinach and Mushroom Lasagne with Cottage Cheese straight from Italy, or a thoroughbred meat eater who thrives on Wine-Braised Venison with Piquant Red Cabbage. Irresistible. Desserts and puddings are sumptuous (which surprised even me), I've managed to come up with healthy cakes and biscuits which taste even better than they look, a Light Salad Dressing without eggs, and some fruity after-dinner petits fours – nibbles if you prefer – which go down a treat with coffee.

The system works beautifully. The food has a satisfying feel to it, it abounds with variety, is packed with vitality and brought down my husband's cholesterol level (way above the normal limit) by 23% in just over three months. Not bad. He's slimmed down nicely, can do up his shoes without puffing and is less fearful of a heart attack than he was before. I joined in too, lost ten pounds in places where it showed and also reduced my own cholesterol. For someone who has already had major heart surgery, relief was sweet.

The cholesterol story? It is difficult, complex to understand and therefore best left to experts like biochemists, nutritionists and cardiologists whose life's work it is and who know exactly what's what medically. But let me put it to you from a layman's point of view. Cholesterol, introduced and recycled by the liver, is essential to life, for the brain and nerves, so let's not knock it too much. Where the heart is concerned though, the picture alters some-what in that there are two kinds of cholesterol which are widely written about in the media: the good and the bad. The bad is LDL which stands for low density lipoproteins. The good, HDL or high density lipoproteins. LDL, gungy, fatty and tenacious, dumps itself in your tissues and more impor-tantly your arteries, then sets about clogging and furring them up, making it difficult for the blood to flow through smoothly. The end result can sometimes lead to a heart attack or stroke. HDL assists in carrying the LDL out of the body, acting like a saucepan brush or kitchen scourer. In fact, a natural cleanser.

FAT

This seems to be the villain of the piece and the message comes across loud and clear with bells on. CUT DOWN ON YOUR OVERALL INTAKE, whatever the source, and don't think one particular kind is a cure-all for cholesterol. It isn't. Now a quick look at the three different fats.

SATURATES

Fats of animal origin like full cream milk and full fat cheese (Cheddar is one example), meat and poultry fat, lard and beef suet.

POLYUNSATURATES

Fats (margarine and oils) of plant origin – sunflower, safflower, corn and grape seed for instance) which keep you on an even keel and won't cause problems, provided you don't eat or use too much.

MONOUNSATURATES

Fruit oil, such as olive, which we know assists HDL "wash" away the more sinister and problematic LDL. Spain has carried out a considerable amount of research into this aspect of cholesterol and the results sound pretty conclusive. Likewise rapeseed oil and fish oils from herring, mackerel, halibut, tuna and salmon. All the oily fish in fact.

Fat aside, you are advised to REDUCE your intake of:

sugar, whatever form it takes

salt

eggs, maximum two a week as the yolks are extremely high in cholesterol.

Having gone through all the rigmarole for the sake of clarity may I suggest you now add spice to life by guzzling your way through the pages of my book with gleeful abandon and enjoy every single minute of it. I promise you've nothing to lose except weight and you'll come out the other side feeling great, looking younger and staying healthy. Give it a go, treat yourself to a multi-vitamin supplement (A to E) on a daily basis and speak to your GP if you are worried or concerned about a change in diet. This applies especially to people with allergies and organic disorders.

CHOLESTEROL GUIDE

DAILY

Feel free to eat any food from the "alphabet" below but keep amounts sensible and portions average.

apples
artichokes
aubergines
baked beans
beer, no more than ½pt/
    275 to 300ml
bread, brown
chestnuts
chicken
cottage cheese, very low fat
chutney
dried peas, beans and lentils
fromage frais

fruit of all kinds, fresh,
    frozen or canned
fruit juice, natural and with
    no added sugar
garlic
ginger
grapefruit
green vegetables
herrings in all forms
jam, diabetic
jelly, low sugar
ketchup
kippers

mackerel in all forms
Marmite
oats and oat bran
olive oil
onions
pasta
pickles
pilchards in sauce
Quark, German, low fat
rice, brown and wild
root vegetables
skimmed milk
sorbet
soups, homemade

salmon, fresh, canned or smoked
spirit, 1 measure
tomato juice
tofu, soy bean curd
trout in all forms
tuna, fresh or canned
turkey
veal
venison
walnuts
white fish
wine, dry, red,1 or 2 glasses
yogurt, low fat and plain

OCCASIONALLY

This stands for once a week.

almonds
avocado, ½ a medium
bacon, lean, small portion
beef, lean, small portion
Brazil nuts
Brie, medium fat
Camembert, medium fat
cashews
cereals, sweet or sugar coated
Edam, medium fat
fish fried without batter
    in polyunsaturated oil
gammon, lean, small portion

golden syrup
hazelnuts
honey
kidney
lamb, lean, small portion
liver
olives
peanut butter, 2 to 3
    teaspoons
pecan nuts
quiche
soup, tinned or packeted
tripe

RARELY

bacon with fat, like streaky
biscuits, except ones in book

cakes, except ones in book
carob

chips
chocolate
coconut
crisps
croissants
duck
goose
fish in batter, deep fried
fizzy sweet drinks
junk food and drinks
lemon curd
macadamia nuts
mayonnaise
milk, full cream and
   semi-skimmed

packeted meats
palm oil
pâtés
pies, fruit and meat
puddings, stodgy, suet kind
roast potatoes
roe of fish, fried or
   as Taramasalata
salad cream, unless
   low fat
salami
sausages
skin of poultry
sweetbreads
tongue

More information may be obtained from:

THE FAMILY HEART ASSOCIATION
9 WEST WAY
BOTLEY
OXFORD OX2 0JB

JOTTINGS

All milk used should be skimmed. Yogurt and fromage frais low fat or very low fat. Margarine, polyunsaturated.

Fromage frais and German Quark are virtually interchangeable.

Although I haven't mentioned it repeatedly throughout the recipes, all fruit, vegetables and herbs should be thoroughly washed before using. Also peeled and trimmed where necessary.

I have avoided including gelatine too often because some people find it problematic and are afraid to use it in case it goes lumpy. Packet jelly has therefore been substituted where appropriate.

Tofu is a high protein food, fatless and mild, which is adaptable and versatile when combined with other foods. It not only takes on their flavours but also adds 'stretch', making the dish go further. It is the colour of milk, tastes deceptively rich and creamy and is widely eaten in China and Japan. It is stocked by health food shops and supermarkets such as Sainsbury and Tesco.

Seasoning is a personal issue and therefore I have left the addition of pepper up to you. Salt substitute may be used in preference to ordinary salt.

When roasting poultry, either conventionally or in the microwave, remove skin and leave UNSTUFFED because fat from the inside would melt and seep into the stuffing.

Venison has the lowest cholesterol content of any flesh food.

To avoid blandness, savoury dishes have been well-seasoned and garlic and other herbs used frequently. If you can't abide garlic, omit completely or substitute mustard.

For speed and convenience, I have used canned beans in the recipes but this doesn't stop you from cooking your own if you prefer. Just remember that ALL BEANS MUST be boiled fairly vigorously for 10 minutes at the beginning to prevent a rather nasty type of food poisoning.

When fresh pasta has been included in a recipe, I have tended to use Dolmio for its high quality and excellent taste. Though it contains egg, the amount is so small that it's not worth worrying about.

Fussell make the handy and convenient skimmed and sweetened condensed milk.

Drilling for oil has produced some beauties. Napolina Golden Light which is a mixture of olive and sunflower oil and mildly flavoured without the intensity of strong-flavoured olive which the British don't always take to. Mazola Light, a 100% pure sunflower oil. From Crete, fairly expensive and not always easy-to-find Candia olive oil with a fine and gentle flavour and well worth seeking out. Vitelma oil, a blend of sunflower, safflower and grapeseed. Meridian Spanish extra virgin olive oil (organic).

Apologies for the non-use of egg yolks which might seem wasteful but they are cholesterol-packed and it's better to give them away to neighbours and friends, who are not watching their diets, than eat them yourself.

If you have high cholesterol and are overweight as well, ration yourself on recipes containing sugar.

Don't be put off by some of the large portions. You'll find because they're fat-free, you won't, or shouldn't, put on weight.

MENU SUGGESTIONS

CHINESE

Thousand Moons Chinese Broth	37
Mixed Vegetable Stir-Fry with Salmon and Walnuts OR	53
Honourable Chicken Wings in Soy Sauce	91
Rice or Noodles	
Braised Chicory with Lemon AND/OR	141
Mixed Bean Salad with Carrot Dressing	125
Canned Lychees or Mandarins	

ENTERTAINING (Formal)

Salmon Dip OR	24
Chestnut and Cranberry Soup OR	38
Marinated and Stuffed Fruit Salad Mushrooms OR	43
Greenland Smoked Halibut Tartar	71
Countrified Turkey Stewpot with Fennel and Herbs	107
Bread Pudding with Brandied Mango Sauce	154

ENTERTAINING (Informal)

Spaghetti with Bright Yellow and Orange Pasta Sauce	122
Very Green Salad	135
Pineapple Rice Pudding with Walnuts	172

EVERYDAY

Turkey Broth with Mixed Vegetables and Barley	29

Smoked Haddock Crumble 66
Seasonal Vegetables or Mixed Salad to Taste
Harvest Fruit Pudding OR 151
Vanilla Jelly Mousse 174

HUNGARIAN

Chicken Paprikás with Yogurt 95
Ribbon Noodles Tossed with Poppy Seeds
Green Salad
Pancakes 178

HOME (UK)

Salmon Cocktails with Seedless Grapes OR 25
Halibut Stuffed Tomatoes 72
Carrot and Orange Soup (optional extra course) 33
Short-Cut Coronation Chicken OR 88
Wine-Braised Pheasant with Prunes and Mustard 111
Mashed or Boiled Potatoes
Figgy OR Ginger Pudding 152 or 150

INDIAN

Dhal Soup 40
Tandoori Chicken OR 96
Chicken Dhansak 93
Vegetable Curry with Chick-Peas 120
Rice and Indian Bread
Raita 143
Tomato, Lettuce and Cucumber Salad
Mango Kulfi OR 174
Eastern Rice Pudding with Rose and Cardamom 169

MEDITERRANEAN

Hot Gazpacho OR	34
Smoky Fish Soup	70
Chicken in Ratatouille	93
Rice or Pasta	
Melon or Figs (fresh or canned)	
Fruit Clusters	185

MIDDLE EASTERN

Meze (hors d'oeuvres) of:	
Aubergine Dip with a Hint of Mint	27
Houmous	47
Minted Cucumber and Fromage Frais Dip	28
Rice Stuffed Vine Leaves	44
Any of the Bulgar recipes	128-132
Apricot and Turkey Kebabs with Mustard Baste on Bed of Rice	104
Purely Vegetarian Stuffed Peppers with Millet (optional)	118
Fresh Fruit	

NORTH EUROPEAN

Rollmops in Sauce with Apples and Gherkins	23
Venison Braise with Red Cabbage	84
Boiled Potatoes	
Baked Mushrooms in their Own Liquor	
Shredded Lettuce Salad tossed with Thick Yogurt	
Orange Cocktails with Soft Fruit Sauce	162

SCANDINAVIAN

Rollmops in Curry Sauce	22

Venison and Turkey Loaf	82
Caraway Cabbage	140
Boiled Potatoes	
Jellied Raspberry Creams	161

TEENAGE

Fishburgers with Salad and Mustard or Ketchup in Sesame Buns	74
Special Slaw with Sunflower Seeds and Herbs	138
Low Fat Fruit Yogurt	

USA

Vichyssoise	42
Cod with Creole Topping OR	64
Fruited Poultry and Nut Salad OR	86
Indoor Barbecue Chicken with Cider Baste	99
Seasonal Vegetables or a big Mixed Salad	
Spiced Sweet Potatoes OR	153
Minted Lemon Meringue Puddings	168

VEGETARIAN

Courgette and Broccoli Soup OR	32
Chilled Mixed Cress Soup	40
Spinach and Mushroom Lasagne with Cottage Cheese	120
Sliced Tomato and Onion Salad seasoned with Fresh Lime Juice	
The Alternative Cheesecake OR	176
Summer Pudding	169

STARTERS

SCANDINAVIAN ROLLMOPS IN CURRY SAUCE

Serves 6

Herrings, in one guise or another, are a national passion in Scandinavia and appear regularly on the gigantic open table, groaning with a complexity of fish, meat, poultry, vegetable dishes and salads. I have simplified this herring dish considerably and swopped fromage frais for the heavy and obligatory mayonnaise. No harm done. Eat with dark rye bread and wash down with a tot or two of schnapps if you have some in the cupboard. Otherwise settle for lager.

1 tblsp medium curry powder
3 tblsp milk
225 to 250g (8oz) fromage frais
4 rollmops with onions, either in a jar or from a delicatessen counter
½ tsp salt
1 tsp Dijon mustard

1 Tip curry powder into a saucepan with the milk. Cook for 1 minute, stirring constantly. You'll notice mixture thickens.

2 Take pan away from heat and stir in fromage frais and drained onions.

3 Cut herrings into bite-sized chunks. Add to pan with salt and mustard.

4 Transfer to a serving dish, cover and refrigerate until quite cold before serving.

ROLLMOPS IN APPLE AND GHERKIN SAUCE

Serves 6 to 8

I first tasted these in Germany over twenty years ago, a cold appetiser of pickled herrings immersed in thick cream with apples and gherkins – immensely rich. I have lightened the load by using fromage frais and the end result remains a success story. Accompany, if you like the taste, with pumpernickel, otherwise opt for rye or straightforward brown bread.

4 large rollmops with onions, either in a jar or bought over the delicatessen counter
225g (8oz) sweet-sour gherkins or pickled cucumbers
225g (8oz) sweet dessert apples like Golden Delicious or Cox
500g (1lb) fromage frais
4 tsp caster sugar

1 Cut rollmops into strips and put into a mixing bowl with onions.

2 Thinly slice gherkins or pickled cucumbers. Peel, core and coarsely chop apples.

3 Add both to rollmops with fromage frais and sugar.

4 Cover and refrigerate lightly before serving in small bowls.

SALMON DIP

Serves 6 to 7

A glutton's dream with dippers of cut-up fresh vegetables, sesame crispbreads or baby new potatoes, still hot and in their skins.

225 to 250g (8oz) smoked salmon trimmings
1 garlic clove, peeled and sliced (optional)
225g (8oz) cottage cheese
1 tblsp lemon juice

1 Put all ingredients into a blender goblet or food processor.

2 Run machine until mixture forms a smooth purée.

3 Scrape into a bowl and serve as suggested.

SALMON COCKTAILS WITH SEEDLESS GRAPES

Serves 6

An up-market starter for entertaining. Serve with crispbreads.

4 tblsp tomato juice
2 tblsp lemon juice
2 tsp Worcestershire sauce
½ tsp salt
125g (4oz) lollo rosso lettuce
350g (12oz) fresh salmon, already cooked
50g (2oz) celery, already cooked
50g (2oz) seedless grapes of any colour

1 Beat the tomato juice with half the lemon juice, Worcestershire sauce and salt.

2 Wash lettuce, drain and coarsely chop. Arrange in 6 stemmed glasses or 6 bowls.

3 Coat with the tomato mixture.

4 Flake salmon. Thinly slice celery. De-stalk grapes. Arrange all three on top of lettuce.

5 Sprinkle with remaining lemon juce, refrigerate briefly and serve within ½ hour of making.

SORREL DIP WITH CRUDITÉS

Serves 8 to 9

A worthwhile proposition when this giant herb, green-leafed and sour, is around, usually in the summer. Spinach will just about do, as will Swiss chard, but the real thing is much more tangy and available by mail order from Rosemary Titterington, herb supplier to grand restaurants and us down here alike. The address is Iden Croft Herbs Ltd., Frittenden Road, Staplehurst, KENT TN12 0DH. Ignore if you grow your own sorrel.

125g (4oz) sorrel
8 spring onions
1 or 2 garlic cloves
450 to 500g (1lb) fromage frais
1 to 1½ tsp salt

1 Wash and dry sorrel and tear leaves into pieces. Trim onions. Peel and slice garlic.

2 Put all three into a blender goblet or food processor with some of the fromage frais.

3 Blend to a smooth but speckly purée, spoon into a bowl and mix in the rest of the fromage frais with salt.

4 Cover and refrigerate about 2 hours before serving with dunks of your choice; cut-up raw vegetables, pieces of apple, baby new potatoes, pieces of crispbread.

AUBERGINE DIP WITH A HINT OF MINT

Serves 8

Sort of Balkan, the dip is exceptionally appetising with warm pieces of pitta or sesame seed bread. Other edible dunks can be made from pieces of fresh fennel, strips of cucumber, short lengths of celery, squares of peppers and chicory leaves. For speed, I cook the aubergines in the microwave.

675 to 700g (1½lb) aubergines
3 tblsp freshly squeezed lemon juice
3 tsp oil
1 garlic clove, peeled and crushed
1½ to 2 tsp salt
225g (8oz) fromage frais
½ tsp concentrated mint sauce

1 Halve aubergines lengthwise and put onto a fairly large plate, cut sides down.

2 Cover with paper towels and cook for 8 minutes at full power in a 650 watt microwave.

3 Scoop pulp out of aubergine shells and transfer to a food processor or blender.

4 Add rest of ingredients then run machine until mixture is smooth and creamy-looking.

5 Spoon into a serving dish and chill lightly before serving.

NOTE:

If you haven't a microwave, arrange aubergine halves on a lightly oiled baking tray, cut sides down. Make a few nicks in the skins, then bake until tender for about 30 to 40 minutes in oven set to 180°C (350°F), Gas 4.

27

MINTED CUCUMBER AND FROMAGE FRAIS DIP

Serves 8

A great refresher in hot weather with dunks of pitta and sesame seed breads.

1 medium cucumber, left unpeeled
225 to 250g (8oz) fromage frais
2 garlic cloves, peeled and crushed
1 tsp salt
2 tsp finely chopped fresh mint or ½ tsp concentrated mint sauce

1 Grate cucumber and wring out in a clean tea towel to remove as much water as possible.

2 Transfer fromage frais to a bowl. Stir in cucumber, garlic, salt and mint.

3 Cover and refrigerate lightly before serving.

TURKEY BROTH WITH MIXED VEGETABLES AND BARLEY

Serves 8 to 10

A warming brew, a complete meal in fact, which I have pressure-cooked to save time. Leftovers can be deep frozen.

2 turkey drumsticks, medium to large
350g (12oz) carrots
225g (8oz) onions
175g (6oz) celery
225g (8oz) spring greens
1 large leek
350g (12oz) tomatoes
75g (3oz) barley
2 to 3 tsp salt
2 litres (3½pt) boiling water
chopped fresh parsley for garnishing

1 Wash and dry drumsticks then skin completely. Put into large pressure cooker.

2 Peel and thinly slice carrots and onions. Wash celery well and cut into thin strips. Wash greens and shred. Trim leek, slit lengthwise, wash well and coarsely shred. Blanch, skin and quarter tomatoes.

3 Place all prepared vegetables into pressure cooker. Mix in barley and salt. Add water, bring to boil and skim.

4 Cover with lid and pressure cook, at full pressure, for 30 minutes.

5 Release pressure. Lift out drumsticks and take meat off bones. Return to pan then reheat and serve in deep bowls with parsley sprinkled thickly over each.

TURKEY COCKTAIL

Serves 6

Straightforward and useful as a Christmas standby when leftover turkey looms large and you have lots of relatives to feed.

350g (12oz) cold cooked turkey
Cocktail Dressing (page 145)
2 Little Gem lettuces or any other lettuce to taste
6 wedges of orange with skin left on to squeeze over cocktails

1 Cut turkey into small cubes, transfer to a mixing bowl and stir in the dressing.

2 Shred washed lettuce and shake dry. Divide between 6 cocktail glasses or glass dishes.

3 Top with equal amounts of turkey mixture and garnish each with a wedge of orange.

EXTRA RED PIMIENTO, BEAN AND TOMATO SOUP

Serves 6

A touch of Mexico here with this zippy summer soup, made at speed in a blender or food processor. Eat with just a few Tortilla chips.

1 can (439g or 15½oz) red kidney beans, undrained
1 can (400g or 14oz) whole pimientos (pickled red peppers), undrained
1 can (400g or 14oz) tomatoes in tomato juice, undrained
1½ tsp salt
300ml (½pt) cold water
1 tsp cumin
1 tblsp Worcestershire sauce
chopped parsley or chopped fresh coriander to garnish

1 Purée first 5 ingredients, in 2 or 3 batches, in a blender goblet or food processor. Leave the texture a bit chunky or smooth, depending on personal taste.

2 Tip into bowl then gently whisk in cumin and Worcestershire sauce.

3 Thin down with a little extra water if soup is too thick.

4 Cover and chill several hours in the fridge before serving. Sprinkle each portion with parsley or coriander.

COURGETTE AND BROCCOLI SOUP

Serves 6

Considering it's made with only four ingredients plus seasoning, the result is a velvety and vibrant moss-green coloured soup, blissfully warming on cold winter evenings. Use frozen vegetables when fresh are unavailable.

450 to 500g (1lb) courgettes
450 to 500g (1lb) broccoli
225g (8oz) onions
750ml (1¼pt) water
1½ to 2 tsp salt
garlic-flavoured croûtons to accompany

1 Wash courgettes and broccoli then thinly slice. Put into saucepan.

2 Coarsely grate onions and add to pan with water and salt.

3 Bring to boil, lower heat and simmer gently for 20 to 25 minutes or until vegetables are tender. Keep pan covered all the time and stir occasionally.

4 Blend half the soup to a smooth purée in a blender goblet or food processor. Add to remainder in pan.

5 Bring back to the boil before serving. Ladle into soup bowls and add 2 to 3 croûtons to each.

CARROT AND ORANGE SOUP

Serves 6

*A trendy soup that looks as if it's here to stay, my gimmick with this one
is to simmer the carrots in carrot juice to intensify the colour and flavour.
It's equally appetising hot or cold and looks attractive when a little set
yogurt is stirred into each portion.*

450 to 500g (1lb) carrots
550ml (18 fluid oz) carrot juice
300ml (½pt) water
1½ tsp salt
1 tblsp cornflour
600ml (1pt) cold milk
1 tsp finely grated orange peel

1 Grate carrots and put into a saucepan with carrot juice, water and salt.

2 Bring to the boil, lower heat and cover. Simmer gently for ¾ hour until
carrots are soft.

3 Blend to a smooth purée in a blender goblet or food processor and return
to pan.

4 Mix cornflour smoothly with some of the milk. Add remainder and pour
into soup. Mix-in orange peel.

5 Cook, stirring all the time, until soup comes to the boil and thickens.
Simmer 2 minutes.

6 Serve hot or cold, with or without yogurt.

HOT GAZPACHO

Serves 6

*A gimmick which works well though you can still have the soup cold as
the Spanish intended. The choice is yours.*

125g (4oz) green pepper
½ medium unpeeled cucumber
75g (3oz) onions
1 can (400g or 14oz) tomatoes in tomato sauce
600ml (1pt) tomato juice
1½ tsp salt
50g (2 oz) fresh brown breadcrumbs
300ml (½pt) water
2 tblsp lemon juice
croûtons for each serving, whether hot or cold

1 Coarsely chop pepper, thickly slice cucumber and cut each onion into
eighths.

2 Transfer to blender goblet or food processor with tomatoes from can. Run
machine until ingredients form a smooth purée, but not too fine.

3 Scrape into a saucepan and add juice from can, tomato juice, salt, crumbs,
water and lemon juice.

4 Heat slowly until soup just comes to the boil. Ladle into bowls and serve
straight away with a few croûtons in each.

5 Alternatively, leave until cold, cover and chill in the refrigerator. Stir
round before serving.

PUMPKIN, LEEK AND APPLE SOUP

Serves 8 to 10

Velvety smooth and golden yellow, nothing could be much more comforting to come home to on a chilly night. The combination of ingredients is unexpected, the flavour gentle and mellow. THE perfect soup for Hallowe'en or Guy Fawkes.

1½kg (3lb) pumpkin
225g (8oz) leek
350g (12oz) dessert apples
600ml (1pt) skimmed milk
3 tsp salt
1 litre (1¾pt) water
½ tsp nutmeg

1 Cut pumpkin into wedges as though it were a melon. Use a strong knife as peel is very tough.

2 Remove peel then cut flesh into small cubes. Put into a large saucepan.

3 Trim leek and cut into thick slices. Peel, core and slice apples. Add both to pumpkin with milk, salt and water.

4 Bring to boil, lower heat and cover. Simmer about 45 minutes or until vegetables are tender.

5 Cool to lukewarm then blend soup to a smooth purée in a blender goblet. Do this in 4 to 5 batches.

6 Return to a clean pan, add nutmeg and reheat until soup just comes up to the boil. Stir from time to time and serve very hot.

DHAL SOUP

Serves 6 to 8

Left unpuréed and with a slice of lemon in each portion, this is a home style soup given to me by a housewife and friend from India. It differs somewhat from restaurant versions in that it is less smooth and more cautiously flavoured – you won't be bowled over by fire. Although not authentic by Indian standards, I add a heaped tablespoon of hot Basmati rice to each serving, thereby transforming the soup into a nutritionally balanced soup or even soup meal, depending on appetite.

225g (8oz) yellow split peas
cold water for soaking
125g (4oz) onions, sliced
1 tsp turmeric
1 tsp cumin
1 tblsp tomato purée
¼ tsp cayenne pepper
2 tsp salt
2 tsp oil
1.25 litres (2¼pt) water
6 to 8 thin slices of lemon
2 tblsp chopped fresh coriander

1 Soak peas overnight in plenty of cold water to cover.

2 Drain and transfer to a large saucepan with all remaining ingredients except last two.

3 Bring to boil, stirring. Lower heat and cover then simmer soup for 1¼ to 1½ hours until peas are very soft and well broken down. Stir frequently to prevent sticking.

4 Ladle into warm soup bowls, add a slice of lemon to each then sprinkle with the coriander.

THOUSAND MOONS CHINESE BROTH

Serves 6

My own kind of oriental creation using Asian vegetables. Add a heaped tablespoon of Chinese noodles to each portion. Delicate and satisfying.

225g (8oz) onions
225g (8oz) Chinese leaves
225g (8oz) fresh bean sprouts
1 can, about 150g (5oz) bamboo shoots, already sliced
1 can, about 150g (5oz) water chestnuts
1 litre (1¾pt) boiling water
1 tblsp soy sauce
½ tsp freshly grated ginger
1 to 1½ tsp salt
8 spring onions
freshly cooked noodles

1 Chop onions. Cut Chinese leaves into thin shreds. Transfer to a large pan with bean sprouts and undrained bamboo shoots.

2 Thinly slice water chestnuts. Add to pan with water, soy sauce, ginger and salt. Bring to boil, lower heat and cover.

3 Simmer 25 minutes. Trim and halve spring onions lengthwise and cut into narrow shreds.

4 Ladle soup into bowls. Add spring onions and noodles to each.

CHESTNUT AND CRANBERRY SOUP

Serves 6

You're either going to like this one or not. No compromise. One friend described it as gravy and where was the beef, another thought it was just the thing to serve at Christmas and wasn't it mild and subtle. There you go.

600ml (1pt) milk
1 can (439g or 15½oz) unsweetened chestnut purée
4 tblsp cranberry sauce
1 vegetable stock cube
450ml (¾pt) hot water
1 tsp salt
2 tsp Dijon mustard

1 Bring milk to the boil in a roomy saucepan. Take off heat then whisk in chestnut purée, bit by bit.

2 Cook gently until boiling, whisking continuously until smooth and thickened.

3 Add cranberry sauce, stock cube dissolved in the water, the salt and mustard.

4 Reheat until hot without boiling. Serve straight away with croûtons.

CLEAR BEETROOT SOUP

Serves 6

Recapture the halcyon days of old Russia with this vivid red beetroot soup, clear as crystal. Pop half a boiled potato into each serving for a modicum of authenticity.

450 to 500g (1lb) cooked beetroots
1.2 litres (2pt) water
4 tblsp fresh strained lemon juice
1 garlic clove, peeled and halved
2 tsp salt

1 Peel and grate beetroots and put two-thirds into a saucepan. Add water, lemon juice, garlic and salt.

2 Bring to the boil, lower heat and cover. Simmer for 45 minutes.

3 Strain and return liquid to pan with rest of beetroots. Bring up to the boil and strain into 6 warm soup bowls.

CHILLED MIXED CRESS SOUP

Serves 6

A beauty for the height of summer and no cooking.

2 tubs of mustard and cress
2 bunches of watercress
500g (1lb) set yogurt
450ml (¾pt) skimmed milk
½ to 1 tsp salt

1 Rinse mustard and cress under cold, running water. Shake dry then cut stalks level to tops of boxes. Put into blender or food processor.

2 Add rinsed watercress, minus stalks.

3 Spoon in about one third of the yogurt and run machine until smooth.

4 Scrape into a large mixing bowl then whisk in remaining yogurt, milk and salt.

5 Cover and refrigerate several hours until thoroughly chilled. Stir round before serving.

CHILLED PLUM, APPLE AND LEMON SOUP

Serves 4

Make when you have spare time to pass this special soup through a fine mesh sieve as in the old days. It makes all the difference to what is a typically central and east European chilled starter, the best thing to happen to scorching summer days.

450 to 500g (1lb) ripe plums
450 to 500g (1lb) cooking apples
narrow strips of peel cut from ½ washed and dried medium lemon
300ml (½pt) cold water
3 tblsp Dubonnet
1 tsp vanilla essence
3 tblsp caster sugar
1 tblsp cornflour
skimmed milk or buttermilk

1 Wash plums then halve and remove stones. Peel, core and slice apples. Put both into a saucepan with the lemon peel and half the water.

2 Cook until tender, keeping pan covered throughout and allow from 10 to 12 minutes. Stir from time to time to prevent fruit catching on base of pan.

3 Stir in Dubonnet, vanilla and sugar. Heat through, stirring.

4 Mix cornflour smoothly with remaining cold water. Add to fruit. Cook, stirring, until soup comes to the boil and thickens.

5 Simmer gently for 2 minutes. Cool to lukewarm then rub through a fine mesh sieve directly into a bowl.

6 Cover when cold and refrigerate until ready to serve. Spoon into 4 bowls and either leave plain or float a little skimmed milk or buttermilk on top.

VICHYSSOISE

Serves 8

*Name French. Origin USA. A classic like no other. This rendering is light
as light, plain yogurt replacing the more customary cream.*

white part of 2 large leeks
125g (4oz) onions
450g (1lb) potatoes (not new ones)
600ml (1pt) vegetable stock, made with cube and water
1½ level tsp salt
1 bouquet garni sachet
½ tsp nutmeg
225g (8oz) yogurt
finely chopped chives for garnishing

1 Trim leeks and thoroughly wash. Cut into chunks. Slice onions. Cut each
potato into eighths. Put all vegetables in a large saucepan.

2 Add stock, salt, bouquet garni and nutmeg. Bring to boil, lower heat and
cover.

3 Simmer 40 to 50 minutes until vegetables are all very soft. Blend, in 3 or
4 batches, in blender goblet or food processor until smooth and creamy.

4 Pour into a bowl and beat in yogurt until all pieces disappear. Cover and
chill several hours in the refrigerator.

5 Before serving, stir round and thin down with a little milk if too thick for
personal taste. Ladle into bowls and sprinkle each with chives.

MARINATED AND STUFFED FRUIT SALAD MUSHROOMS

Serves 4

A starter with a difference, dark and handsome, an attraction when arranged on individual plates lined with radicchio, lamb's lettuce or mustard and cress sprinkled with lemon juice.

4 large, flat mushrooms, each 10 to 13cm (4 to 5in) across
2 tblsp tomato ketchup
1 tblsp wine vinegar
1 tsp Worcestershire sauce
1 tblsp water
75g (3oz) tomatoes
125g (4oz) dessert pears, peeled
25g (1oz) celery
2 tblsp chopped parsley
225g (8oz) cottage cheese with added pineapple
slices of peeled kiwi fruit or watercress for garnishing

1 Trim mushrooms and remove stalks then rinse and wipe dry with paper towels. Arrange, in single layer, on a large plate, flat for preference.

2 Put ketchup, vinegar, Worcestershire sauce and water into a small saucepan. Bring just up to the boil, stirring.

3 Spoon over mushrooms and refrigerate 3 to 4 hours.

4 Before serving, coarsely chop tomatoes, pears and celery.

5 Transfer to bowl and stir in parsley and cheese.

6 Stand mushrooms on 4 lettuce or cress lined plates. Pile cheese mixture over each then garnish with kiwi or watercress.

RICE STUFFED VINE LEAVES

Serves 6

Usually quite oily, I have compromised and used only 2 teaspoons, turning this into a low cholesterol starter to go with other Middle Eastern dishes such as Houmous and any of the bulgar mixes. It is more labour intensive than some of the other recipes so you need patience.

1 packet (225g/250g or 8oz) vine leaves in brine
boiling and cold water
150g (5oz) uncooked, long grain rice
175g (6oz) tomatoes
75g (3oz) onions
50g (2oz) raisins
1 tsp mixed spice
2 tblsp finely chopped parsley
2 tblsp finely chopped mint
¼ to ½ tsp salt

TOPPING
150ml (¼pt) hot water
juice of ½ lemon
1 tsp icing sugar
2 tsp olive oil
1 garlic clove, peeled and sliced (optional)

1 Soak vine leaves in a large bowl of boiling water for 20 to 30 minutes as this reduces saltiness. Drain and cover with cold water. Leave to soak 4 to 5 hours.

2 Meanwhile cook rice in boiling salted water as directed on the packet. Drain if necessary then fluff up with a fork.

3 Chop tomatoes into smallish pieces. Whether you remove seeds or not is up to you – I don't. Peel and chop onions. Fork both into rice with raisins, spice, parsley, mint and salt.

4 Drain vine leaves in a colander. Separate with great care (as they tend to tear easily) and place flat on two tea towels.

5 Line base of fairly large saucepan with the least good looking leaves; even broken ones will do.

6 Put a little rice filling on remaining leaves and roll each up tightly, completely enclosing filling.

7 With joins underneath, arrange in a single layer in prepared saucepan.

8 For topping, combine water with lemon juice, sugar and oil. Pour over the vine rolls and dot here and there with the garlic if used.

9 Bring to boil, lower heat and cover. Simmer gently for 1½ hours, topping up with extra boiling water every now and then to prevent pan from boiling dry.

10 Transfer to a serving dish when cold. Cover and refrigerate 1 to 2 hours before serving.

GLOBE ARTICHOKES WITH TWO SAUCES

Serves 4

Globe artichokes, shaped like water lilies but with their leaves more closely and tightly packed together, are basically an edible thistle and were the height of fashion during the reign of Henry VIII. Since then they have spread their wings throughout the UK and emerged as a summer delicacy, imported from Brittany for the most part, with just the right degree of lightness to set off a lunch or dinner to perfection. For serving, do provide finger bowls, each half-filled with water and a slice of lemon, as artichokes are mostly tackled with the hands.

4 globe artichokes
cold salted water
10cm (4 inch) boiling water
1 tsp salt

GOLDEN SAUCE WITH CARROT JUICE
125g (4oz) fromage frais
2 tsp Dijon mustard
1 tblsp carrot juice
¼ tsp salt

SPIKY TOMATO SAUCE
2 tblsp tomato ketchup
½ tsp sesame oil
1 tblsp lemon juice
2 tblsp yogurt
2 tblsp milk

1 To prepare artichokes, remove stems and, for a professional finish, cut off tips of leaves with kitchen scissors.

2 Soak artichokes for 30 minutes in cold salted water. Drain thoroughly then stand upright and close together in a saucepan.

3 Mix boiling water and salt together and pour into pan. Bring back to boil, cover and simmer 45 minutes.

4 Drain upside down and leave to cool. To eat, peel off one leaf at a time and dip the base in either of the two sauces (below). Pass between the teeth then throw away rest of inedible leaf.

5 Keep going until you come to a cone of leaves in the middle. Lift off and discard then pull out all the spikey 'choke'.

6 You've now reached the heart – the best part. Cover with sauce and eat with a knife and fork.

7 To make either sauce, beat all ingredients for each well together with a fork and transfer to small dishes.

HOUMOUS

Serves 6 to 8

Usually part of the Balkan and Middle Eastern meze table (hors d'oeuvres), eat this creamy-textured sesame seed and chick-pea paste with warm pitta bread or baby new potatoes, freshly cooked. The Houmous makes a marvellous salad dressing and can also be used to replace margarine as a spread on bread or crispbreads.

1 can (440g or 15oz) chick-peas in water
½ jar (170g or 6oz) Tahini (sesame seed paste), well-stirred to distribute oil
1 garlic clove, peeled and sliced
4 tblsp lemon juice
½ tsp salt

1 Tip chick-peas and liquor from can into a food processor or blender goblet.

2 Add tahini, garlic, lemon juice and salt.

3 Blend to a smooth purée, thinning down with a little water if too thick for personal taste.

FISH

PUMPKIN WITH SAUTÉED SMOKED SALMON, GARLIC AND SESAME

Serves 4

A flamboyant gathering, destined for high places. The blissful thing about smoked salmon is that it can be sautéed in its own natural oil, making additional fat unnecessary. With some garlic and crisp sesame seeds, it converts into a super main course with freshly-cooked orange pumpkin cubes – smoky-tasting and quite a curiosity. For contrast, serve with green noodles or spaghetti.

1½kg (3lb) pumpkin
boiling salted water
350g (12oz) smoked salmon trimmings
1 garlic clove, peeled and crushed
50g (2oz) sesame seeds

1 Cut pumpkin into wedges as though it were a melon. This is tough work so use a strong knife.

2 Remove peel then cut flesh into small cubes. Cook in boiling salted water for about 20 minutes or until tender, keeping heat moderate and pan half covered.

3 Meanwhile cut salmon into cubes or strips and gently sauté in a frying pan until hot.

4 Add garlic and sesame seeds then continue to sauté for a few minutes longer until salmon looks cooked and seeds begin to turn golden.

5 Drain pumpkin, return to pan and gently stir in salmon mixture. Either transfer to a warm dish for serving or put directly on to 4 warm plates.

BROWN SPAGHETTI WITH SMOKED SALMON AND SPRING ONIONS

Serves 2 to 3

A top drawer main course and one which can be made at reasonable cost from salmon trimmings. Accompany with a green salad.

225g (8oz) slim brown spaghetti
boiling salted water
225g (8oz) smoked salmon trimmings
8 medium-sized spring onions
salt and freshly-milled pepper to taste
2 tsp grated Parmesan cheese

1 Cook spaghetti in boiling salted water as directed on the packet.

2 Meanwhile, cut salmon into strips. Trim spring onions and coarsely chop.

3 Drain spaghetti thoroughly and return to saucepan. Add salmon with onions and seasoning to taste. Toss well with 2 forks.

4 Transfer to plates and sprinkle each serving lightly with cheese.

BAKED FRESH SALMON FILLET IN TOASTED CRUMBS WITH POPPY SEEDS

Serves 6

With farmed salmon available all the year round and more economically priced than it used to be, this is top level stuff for fish lovers. Serve with any of the fashionable 'browns'; rice, pasta or jacket potatoes split and filled with cottage cheese and chives.

1 salmon fillet (one side) weighing about 500 to 750g (between 1¼ and 1½lb) and cut
from a medium-sized whole fish
1 egg white from Grade 2 egg
6 to 7 tblsp brown toasted breadcrumbs
salt, pepper and poppy seeds for sprinkling
fronds of fresh dill for garnishing

1 Set oven to 220°C (425°F), Gas 7.

2 Skin salmon, or ask fishmonger to do this for you, then cut flesh into 6 even-sized pieces.

3 Beat egg white until foamy. Tip crumbs on to a piece of foil.

4 Coat fish with egg white then toss in crumbs until each portion is evenly-covered. Sprinkle with salt, pepper and poppy seeds.

5 Transfer to a lightly oiled, shallow baking tin and bake for 15 to 20 minutes. To serve, garnish each portion with dill.

MIXED VEGETABLE STIR-FRY WITH FRESH SALMON AND WALNUTS

Serves 4

An adventurous stir-fry, perfect with oriental noodles.

450 to 500g (1lb) fresh salmon, cut from tail-end and filleted
175g (6oz) Chinese leaves
50g (2oz) button mushrooms
50g (2oz) red pepper
1 tblsp oil
175g (6oz) bean sprouts
125g (4oz) baby sweetcorn, fresh or canned
1 garlic clove, peeled and crushed
50g (2oz) walnuts, chopped
1 tblsp cornflour
4 tblsp cold water
2 tsp soy sauce
2 tsp Worcestershire sauce
1 tblsp ginger wine
½ tsp salt

1 Wash and dry salmon, remove skin and cut flesh into narrow strips.

2 Shred Chinese leaves. Thinly slice mushrooms and pepper.

3 Heat oil until sizzling in heavy frying pan or wok. Add all the vegetables, garlic and nuts then stir-fry for 10 minutes, tossing ingredients over and over all the time.

4 Add salmon and stir-fry for 5 minutes.

5 To thicken, mix cornflour smoothly with all remaining ingredients including salt.

6 Add to salmon mixture and stir-fry, tossing gently, until ingredients are shiny and liquid thickened. Serve straight away with hot noodles.

SALMON AND POTATO MERINGUE PIE

Serves 4 to 5

A nice, comfortable family main course, fun for children with frozen peas and ketchup on the side – what else!

700g (1½lb) potatoes
boiling salted water
1 can (439g or 15oz) pink salmon
1 tsp prepared English mustard
1 tsp salt
4 tblsp finely chopped chives or spring onions
2 egg whites
pinch of salt

1 Cut up potatoes and cook in boiling salted water until soft. Drain and finely mash.

2 Set oven to 220°C (425°F), Gas 7. Drain salmon, reserving 3 tablespoons of liquor from can. Mash fish and add to potatoes with liquor.

3 Stir in mustard, salt and chives or chopped onions. Spread evenly into a 20cm (8 inch) round and lightly greased heatproof dish, about 5cm (2 inches) in depth.

4 Cover with foil and heat through for 30 to 35 minutes.

5 Beat egg whites to a stiff snow with salt. Take dish out of the oven, uncover and pile meringue over the top.

6 Reheat 5 to 7 minutes until meringue is lightly tipped with gold. Eat straight away.

PASTA SHELL SALAD WITH TUNA AND COFFEE-SOAKED RAISINS

Serves 4

An odd-ball collection of ingredients, healthy and wholesome. Eat with sliced tomatoes and crispbreads.

50g (2oz) raisins
3 tblsp strong black coffee
50g (2oz) walnuts
225g (8oz) pasta shells
boiling salted water
1 can (200g or 7oz) tuna in oil
2 tblsp lemon juice
1 level tsp dried oregano or 1 tblsp chopped fresh
50g (2oz) onion
125g (4oz) cooked chicken
125g (4oz) cooked sweetcorn
lettuce for lining salad bowl

1 Put raisins into a small dish, add coffee and leave to soak for 4 to 5 hours. Toss from time to time.

2 Lightly toast walnuts then finely chop.

3 Cook pasta in the boiling salted water until just tender; about 7 minutes. Drain well and transfer to a mixing bowl.

4 Mash up tuna in its own oil then add to pasta with lemon juice and oregano.

5 Finely grate onion. Cut chicken into strips. Add both, with the sweetcorn, to the salad.

6 Drain raisins. Gently mix into salad with half the walnuts.

7 Spoon salad into a lettuce-lined bowl and sprinkle rest of nuts over the top.

WHOLEMEAL PIZZA WITH COTTAGE CHEESE AND SALMON

Serves 8 generously

I've had mixed reactions from people over this one. They either like the wholemeal base or they don't (it's an unyeasted one) though the topping has come in for no criticism whatever, as far as my own family is concerned. It's one of our stand-bys and is great for a quickly-prepared supper when an unexpected gathering of friends turn up without warning. I speak from experience.

BASE
2 tblsp salad oil
450g (1lb) wholemeal self-raising flour
1 tsp baking powder
1 tsp dried basil
450ml (¾pt) milk

TOPPING
2 cans (each 400g or 14oz) chopped tomatoes
garlic salt
1 can (439g or 15½oz) red or pink salmon, drained
1 can (about 400g or 14oz) sweet red peppers
350g (12oz) cottage cheese
1 can (50g or 2oz) anchovies in oil OR 2 tblsp drained capers

1 Well-oil a large roasting tin measuring 39 by 35cm (about 15 by 14 inch). Set oven to 220°C (450°F), Gas 7.

2 Tip flour into a bowl. Toss in baking powder and basil then add all the milk in one go.

3 Draw together with a fork, knead BRIEFLY until smooth then stand in middle of tin.

4 With floured hands, ease dough across base, slightly raising edges (this is quickly done).

5 Cover with tomatoes almost to edges, sprinkle to taste with garlic salt (or onion if preferred) then dot here and there with flakes of salmon.

6 Drain peppers and cut into strips. Arrange on top of pizza with cheese and anchovies or capers.

7 Bake 30 to 35 minutes until topping begins to bubble. Remove from oven, cut into wedges and serve straight away.

LUCY'S PORTUGUESE LEMON AND TUNA CASSEROLE WITH THREE VEGETABLES

Serves 4

A refreshingly edible speciality from Portugal, passed on to me by one of the staff at our local medical centre. Lucy discovered it on holiday and it's an ingenious way of using fresh tuna, a fairly dry fish, to advantage. Cost-wise it's expensive because the fish has to be flown here from afar.

175g (6oz) onions
1 garlic clove, peeled and crushed
2 tblsp oil
450g (1lb) firm tomatoes
450g (1lb) potatoes
salt and pepper to taste
750g (1½lb) fresh tuna
2 large lemons
½ teacup chopped fresh coriander

1 Set oven to 220°C (425°F), Gas 7.

2 Peel onions and finely chop. Fry, with garlic, in the oil until pale and gold. Keep heat moderate to prevent burning. Leave aside for the time being.

3 Blanch and skin tomatoes then cut into wedges. Peel potatoes, wash well, thinly slice and dry thoroughly.

4 Layer onions, garlic, tomatoes and potatoes in a 2¾ litre (5 pint) ungreased casserole dish, sprinkling salt and pepper between the layers.

5 Skin tuna, cut into chunks and arrange on top of vegetables. Wash and dry lemons, thinly slice and use to cover fish. Sprinkle with coriander.

6 Cover with lid or foil and cook 1¼ hours, uncovering for the last 30 minutes. Serve piping hot with green vegetables.

TOMATO AND TUNA BREAD SLICE PIZZA

Serves 4

Why go to the bother of making a pizza base when bread slices will do just as well? This one is directed at young families as it should appeal to teenagers and parents alike. See what you think.

4 by 1cm (½ inch) slices of bread, cut LENGTHWISE from a small brown loaf
150g (5oz) tomato purée
1 tsp caster sugar
½ tsp salt
1 garlic clove, peeled and crushed
1 tsp dried basil
450g (1lb) tomatoes, blanched and skinned
75g (3oz) onions
4 heaped tblsp chopped pickled peppers
1 can (200g or 7oz) tuna chunks, drained
16 green olives, without stones
24 capers (optional)
4 rounded tsp grated Parmesan cheese

1 Set oven to 230°C (450°F), Gas 8.

2 Arrange bread slices on a large baking tray.

3 Mix together purée, sugar, salt, garlic and basil. Spread evenly over bread.

4 Chop tomatoes and onions. Spoon on top of the purée with the peppers.

5 Top with flakes of tuna then decorate with the olives and capers if used.

6 Sprinkle with the cheese then heat through and brown in the oven for about 10 to 12 minutes.

BAKED HERRINGS WITH BROWN BREAD AND ORANGE STUFFING

Serves 4

Good for you, piquant and economical, just the thing for winter when herrings are at their most succulent – plump, tender and sweetly-flavoured. Serve with boiled potatoes sprinkled with chopped watercress.

4 large herrings
125g (4oz) brown bread
125g (4oz) onions
½ tsp salt
2 tsp tarragon vinegar
1 tsp Dijon mustard
1 tsp finely grated orange peel
1 tsp oil

1 Set oven to 200°C (400°F), Gas 6.

2 Ask fishmonger to remove heads from herrings and take out backbones.

3 Wash and dry fish. For stuffing, convert bread into crumbs and tip into mixing bowl.

4 Chop onions finely and add to crumbs with salt, vinegar, mustard and orange peel.

5 Divide stuffing equally down the length of each herring then hold flaps of fish together with small metal skewers or thick wooden cocktail sticks.

6 Arrange in small roasting tin lined with greaseproof or non-stick baking paper, brush with the oil and bake 30 minutes.

ANNIE'S HERRING STEW

Serves 4 to 6

The origins of this peasanty fish dish remain obscure but it was cooked by my mother, a practical, unpretentious and down-to-earth person, on a semi-regular basis during childhood days and dished up in deep, secure bowls with big soup spoons. I remember it fondly, not very beautiful but immensely sustaining and cheering to heart and mind on very cold days after school. But to stay out of trouble, I always heeded my mother's repeated warning, "mind the bones". I urge you to do the same.

700g (1½lb) potatoes
350g (12oz) onions
600ml (1pt) water
2 tsp salt
6 large herrings, cleaned and filleted
5 tblsp chopped parsley

1 Slice potatoes fairly thickly. Repeat with onions. Transfer to a roomy saucepan.

2 Add water and salt. Bring to boil, lower heat and cover. Simmer about 30 minutes until both vegetables are soft. It doesn't matter if they break up a little bit – it's characteristic of the dish.

3 Wash herrings and cut into chunks, removing fins at the same time. Mix into vegetables and cook no more than 5 minutes.

4 Ladle into large, warm soup bowls, sprinkle each thinly with parsley and serve piping hot.

SMOKED MACKEREL PÂTÉ LOAF IN PARSLEY CLOAK

Serves 6 to 8

A touch of heaven – if you like smoked mackerel – with fresh hot toast or crisp brown rolls. This nutritious and low fat pâté has all the panache associated with gourmet cooking and should appeal to lowbrows and highbrows in our gastronomic midst.

350g (12oz) smoked mackerel fillet
225g (8oz) skimmed milk soft cheese
1 tsp coarse grain mustard
1 tsp Worcestershire sauce
50g (2oz) walnuts
25 to 30g (1oz) fresh parsley, weighed without stalks
lemon wedges

1 Take mackerel off its skin and flake up the flesh with two forks. It doesn't have to be too fine.

2 Tip cheese into a bowl and, using a fork, gradually work in the mackerel, mustard and Worcestershire sauce.

3 Cover and refrigerate thoroughly until firm.

4 To complete, chop nuts and parsley very finely together. Tip on to a piece of foil to form an even layer.

5 Put the mackerel mixture on top, shaping it into a 20cm (8 inch) roll. Cover thickly with the parsley and nuts, making sure there are no thin patches.

6 Re-wrap carefully in a double piece of clean foil and twist ends. The roll should now look like a Christmas cracker.

7 Refrigerate until firm, unwrap and stand on an oblong plate for serving. Cut in slices. Accompany each portion with lemon.

LEMON MARINATED KIPPER WITH ONION

Serves 4 to 5

Many years ago, when I ran a cookery test kitchen for an advertising agency, one of my elder and wiser colleagues advocated using thin slices of raw kipper fillet as a topping for toast or a sandwich filling. Nutritionally sound, this became an office classic at lunchtime and all I've done here is to up-date what remains a sound and appetising idea.

350g (12oz) raw kipper fillet
strained juice of 1 medium lemon
50g (2oz) onion

1 Cut kipper flesh into thin slices and put into a bowl. Coat with the lemon juice.

2 Cut onion into hair thin slices. Add to kipper, mix in well then cover. Leave to marinate in the fridge for 6 to 8 hours.

3 Drain fish and onion. Transfer to dish and eat as snack with crispbreads, toast or Continental rye bread. The little bones in the fish, by the way, seem to melt away in the lemon juice.

COD WITH CREOLE TOPPING

Serves 4

*Full of good healthy vegetables covering portions of light and flaky cod,
this has turned out to be a colourful contribution from the deep south of
the USA. It goes beautifully with sweetcorn and brown rice.*

675g (1½lb) cod fillet, skinned
350g (12oz) tomatoes, blanched and skinned
125g (4oz) EACH:
green pepper
onions
celery
fresh okra

1 tblsp oil
1 tsp salt
3 tblsp crisp brown breadcrumbs

1 Set oven to 200°C (400°F), Gas 6.

2 Wash and dry fish then cut into 4 portions. Arrange, in a single layer, in
an ovenproof dish (not too deep).

3 Chop tomatoes and leave on one side for the time being.

4 De-seed pepper and coarsely chop the flesh. Peel onions and coarsely
grate. Cut celery into thin, diagonal strips. Top and tail okra then cut each
into 5 chunks.

5 Sizzle oil in a large saucepan. Add all prepared vegetables except
tomatoes. Fry gently for 15 minutes, stirring occasionally. Mix in tomatoes
and salt.

6 Spoon over fish, sprinkle with crumbs and cook, uncovered, for 30
minutes.

BUCKWHEAT KEDGEREE WITH SMOKED COD

Serves 4 to 6

Usually made with rice, buckwheat adds its own earthiness to a well-established breakfast classic, now more appropriate for lunch, supper or brunch. Instead of hard boiled eggs, I have used cottage cheese in order to add the typical speckles associated with chopped whites.

225g (8oz) buckwheat
450ml (¾pt) boiling water
1 tsp salt
450 to 500g (1lb) smoked cod fillet
2 tsp margarine
225g (8oz) cottage cheese
fromage frais for topping or yogurt if preferred
4 heaped tblsp chopped parsley

1 Put buckwheat into a saucepan with water and salt. Bring to boil, lower heat and cover. Simmer 30 minutes.

2 In a deep pan, poach cod in cold water for about 8 minutes or until tender, changing water twice to reduce saltiness. Drain and flake.

3 Drain buckwheat if necessary then stir in fish, margarine, cottage cheese and two-thirds of the parsley.

4 Heat through until hot, keeping heat low and stirring from time to time to prevent sticking.

5 Spoon out on to plates and top each portion with a dollop of fromage frais or yogurt and a sprinkling of parsley.

SMOKED HADDOCK CRUMBLE

Serves 4 to 5

Unpretentious and all the better for it with hot mash and mushy peas,
canned or frozen and freshly cooked.

450 to 475g (1lb) smoked haddock fillet
cold water
1 tblsp cornflour
300ml (½pt) cold milk
1 tsp prepared English mustard
salt to taste
15g (½oz) dry toasted brown breadcrumbs

CRUMBLE
75g (3oz) half fat Cheddar cheese
1 tblsp dry toasted breadcrumbs

1 Set oven to 220°C (425°F), Gas 7.

2 Poach haddock for 10 minutes in cold water, changing water twice to reduce saltiness. Drain and flake.

3 To make 2-step sauce without soiling too many utensils, tip cornflour into a saucepan and blend smoothly with a little cold milk.

4 Whisk in remainder and slowly bring to the boil, stirring all the time, until sauce comes to the boil and thickens.

5 Simmer 2 minutes, add fish and mustard then season to taste with salt if necessary. Stir in crumbs.

6 Spoon into a 1 litre (1¾ pint) lightly greased pie dish, spread evenly with a knife then sprinkle top with cheese and crumbs.

7 Reheat 10 to 15 minutes until browned and bubbly and serve piping hot.

PLAICE FOLD-OVERS WITH SALMON FILLING

Serves 4

Canned fish inside fresh is a novel idea if not a unique one and in this instance the result is a pretty apricot and white main course which looks a bit like Italian marble. It's fun with white rice smothered with chopped parsley or chives and either lightly cooked seasonal vegetables or a full blown salad. It's been designed for the microwave.

4 large plaice fillets, each about 225 to 250g (8oz)
75g (3oz) fresh breadcrumbs, white or brown
125g (4oz) onions
75g (3oz) sweet-sour pickled cucumber
1 can (200g or 7oz) red salmon
4 tsp creamed horseradish
paprika

1 Wash and dry fish and spread out on a piece of foil, skin sides uppermost.

2 Tip crumbs into a bowl. Chop onions finely, repeat with cucumber then add both to crumbs.

3 Mash in salmon and liquor from can then use equal amounts to cover half of each plaice fillet.

4 Fold over then arrange in a 23cm (9 inch) dish to about 5cm (2 inches) in depth.

5 Spread with the horseradish then sprinkle with paprika.

6 Cover with cling film, nick twice and cook 25 minutes at defrost setting in a 650 watt microwave oven.

DEVILY PILCHARD SPREAD

Serves 6

A tongue-teaser of a sandwich filling or topping for hot toast, the spread is in the budget category and nutritious with it.

1 can (425g or 15oz) pilchards in tomato sauce
75g (3oz) onions
1 tblsp Worcestershire sauce
2 tsp whole grain mustard powder
1 tsp medium curry powder

1 Finely mash pilchards in their own sauce.

2 Grate onions on fine side of grater. Stir into fish with remaining ingredients.

3 Mix thoroughly. Cover and refrigerate up to 1 day.

ROYAL GREENLAND HALIBUT

Quite outstanding, fairly new on the scene and rich in important and protective omega 3 and omega 6 fish oils, this is a luxurious fish with, understandably, a price tag to match. Available on the Continent for years now, it is becoming more generally available in the UK from top food shops and is well worth seeking out. Like smoked salmon it is sold already sliced. Three recipes follow.

SMOKY FISH SOUP

Serves 4 to 5

Total and utter extravagance is the name of the game here – a wonderful experience wrapped in Mediterranean warmth and colour. Eat with warm and crusty French bread for a main dish like no other and accompany with lightly chilled Muscadet. Memorable.

2 garlic cloves
225g (8oz) onions
1 can (400g or 12oz) tomatoes in tomato juice
300ml (½pt) water
1 tsp sugar
6 to 8 saffron strands
500g (just over 1lb) monkfish
225g (8oz) Royal Greenland smoked halibut
250ml (8 fluid oz) dry white wine
1 tsp herbes de Provence
1 tsp finely grated orange peel

1 Peel garlic and crush directly into a saucepan. Thinly slice onions and add to pan with tomatoes and juice from can, the water, sugar and saffron.

2 Bring to the boil, crushing down tomatoes with the back of a spoon. Lower heat, cover and simmer gently for 1½ hours.

3 Cut monkfish into scampi sized pieces. Cut halibut into squares or strips.

4 Add to tomato mixture with wine, herbes and orange peel.

5 Bring to boil and reduce heat. Leave uncovered and simmer 5 minutes. Ladle into deep bowls and serve very hot.

SMOKED HALIBUT TARTAR

Serves 6

Exceptionally tasty with fingers of hot toast or crispbreads, the Tartar is loosely based on the once-upon-a-time Russian classic made with raw beef and surrounded by assorted condiments plus an egg yolk. It was meant to be a DIY cavalcade but in my adaptation all the ingredients have been mixed in for you and the egg yolks excluded for obvious reasons. An enjoyable luxury for lunch or supper.

75g (3oz) onion
450g (1lb) Royal Greenland smoked halibut
1 tblsp lemon juice
2 tblsp finely chopped fennel fronds (the herb, not the bulb)
2 tsp finely chopped chervil or celery
1 tsp Dijon mustard
1 tblsp drained capers

1 Grate or finely chop onion. Repeat with halibut but chop a little more coarsely.

2 Put both into a mixing bowl and work in lemon juice, fennel, chervil or celery and the mustard.

3 Turn into a serving dish and sprinkle with capers. Eat at room temperature.

HALIBUT STUFFED TOMATOES

Serves 4

Smoked halibut in this instance makes a superb substitute for prawns and the sweetness of the eating apples adds just the right touch of subtlety.

4 medium-sized beef tomatoes, about 1kg (2lb)
125g (4oz) Royal Greenland smoked halibut
150g (5oz) dessert apples
25g (1oz) toasted brown breadcrumbs
1 tblsp lemon juice
dried dill weed or chopped fresh dill for garnishing

1 Halve the tomatoes and remove centres with a curved grapefruit knife, taking care not to pierce the skins.

2 Chop tomato centres finely and put into a bowl. Cut halibut into strips and add.

3 Peel, core and dice apple. Combine with tomato mixture then stir in crumbs and lemon juice.

4 Return to tomato halves and sprinkle each with dill. Transfer to a flat plate, cover and refrigerate for about 2 hours.

5 Remove from the fridge about 1 hour before serving and sprinkle each one with dill. Eat for lunch or supper or keep as a starter.

MIXED VEGETABLE AND FISH CASSEROLE WITH OAT TOPPING

Serves 4

An easy eater, especially for those who appreciate fish. It's a complete meal in itself.

450 to 500g (1lb) potatoes
350g (12oz) onions
225g (8oz) sliced runner beans or slender topped and tailed French beans
1 tsp salt
2 tsp French mustard
450 to 500g (1lb) smoked haddock fillet
1 tblsp porridge oats

1 Set oven to 230°C (450°F), Gas 8.

2 Thinly slice potatoes and onions then put into a large saucepan with beans.

3 Add boiling water to cover and the salt. Bring to boil, lower heat and cover. Boil steadily for 10 minutes.

4 Drain and transfer to a 20cm (8 inch) round ovenproof dish, about 5cm (2 inches) in depth, lightly brushed with oil.

5 Dot here and there with the mustard. Cut fish into cubes and arrange on top of vegetables.

6 Sprinkle with oats then reheat and brown for about 15 minutes.

FISH BURGERS

Makes 4

Any day as good as the meat ones, slip the hot burgers into warm sesame buns with ketchup or mild mustard.

75g (3oz) soft grain bread with oats
450 to 500g (1lb) filleted and skinned white fish (coley, haddock, cod)
15g (½oz) parsley
75g (3oz) onions, quartered
1 tsp salt
2 tsp oil
1 tblsp water

1 Mince bread and put into a bowl. Cube fish and also mince with parsley and onions. Mix well with the bread.

2 Fork in oil, salt and water, shape into 4 burgers then transfer to a grill pan, lined with foil and lightly oiled.

3 Cook 7 to 10cm (3 to 4 inches) below hot grill, allowing about 10 minutes and turning twice.

4 Burgers are ready when they turn a warm golden brown.

MEAT

BEEF AND TOFU BALLS IN RED HOT LENTIL SAUCE

Serves 6 to 8

The name gives the game away. The meat balls are respectfully hot, teasingly spicy and nestle in a gloriously vibrant orange-coloured sauce. Keep on hand for family and entertaining and serve with brown rice and any favourite salad to taste. Or offer a selection of lightly cooked fresh green vegetables.

350g (12oz) orange lentils
3 tsp tandoori spice mix
1 garlic clove, peeled and crushed
900ml (1½pt) boiling water
2 tsp salt
2 tsp ground cumin

MEAT BALLS
142g (5oz) tofu, drained
450g (1lb) lean ground beef
2 to 8 drops Tabasco (for added heat)
1 garlic clove, peeled and crushed
1 tsp salt
3 tblsp wholewheat semolina

1 Wash lentils in sieve and tip into large pan, more shallow than deep. Add tandoori spice mix, garlic, water, salt and cumin.

2 Bring to boil, stirring constantly, then lower heat and cover. Simmer 15 minutes, stirring three times.

3 Meanwhile, mash tofu finely in a bowl. Add all remaining ingredients and fork-mix until evenly combined.

4 Shape into 24 balls with damp hands and carefully drop into lentil mixture.

5 Bring back to boil, reduce heat and, using a spoon, toss each ball gently over in lentil sauce.

6 Keep mixture simmering, cover again and cook a further 15 minutes.

BEEF PIE WITH CHESTNUTS AND POTATO SLICES

Serves 6

Chestnuts have a superlative thickening quality and in this recipe also 'stretch' the meat, enabling it to serve 6 people generously. It's another of my microwave specials and I can get a meal on the table in about 30 minutes flat. Not bad. Shredded and quickly cooked green cabbage makes a friendly companion.

450 to 500g (1lb) very lean ground beef
1 can (439g or 15½oz) unsweetened chestnut purée
300ml (½pt) boiling water
3 tblsp dried onion flakes
3 tblsp dried mushrooms
1 tsp salt
350g (12oz) cooked new potatoes in their skins

1 Arrange mince in a 20cm (8 inch) dish of about 5cm (2 inch) in depth.

2 Cover with cling film, slit twice and cook for 10 minutes at full power in a 650 watt microwave oven.

3 Uncover and mash in chestnut purée then gradually work in water, dried onion and mushroom flakes, and salt.

4 Slice potatoes fairly thickly and arrange on top of pie. Cover as before and continue to cook for a further 15 minutes. Stand 5 minutes before serving.

VEAL STIR-FRY WITH CHICORY AND RADISHES

Serves 2

With rice or noodles, the stir-fry makes a pretty Chinese picture, albeit imitation, but just right for 2 people.

225g (8oz) veal
1 garlic clove, peeled and crushed
10 large radishes
2 heads of chicory
1 tblsp cornflour
8 tblsp water
2 tsp oriental sesame oil
2 tsp teriyaki sauce
½ tsp salt

1 Finely mince veal and put into a wok or frying pan with the garlic. Dry-fry for 5 minutes, stirring frequently.

2 Meanwhile, trim radishes and chicory and slice both thinly. Add to veal and stir-fry for 5 minutes.

3 Blend cornflour smoothly with water then mix in remaining ingredients.

4 Pour over veal, bring to the boil and simmer 3 minutes, stirring and tossing all the time.

VEAL MARENGO

Serves 4 to 6

An old-established Italian classic we seem to have lost sight of over the years. A pity. Once served to Napoleon (or so the story goes) after the battle of Marengo in Northern Italy, the veal is simmered with tomatoes and mushrooms, flavoured with onions and finally spiked with Marsala. Mine is a lazy version which I serve with easy-cook Italian brown rice or white, depending on availability and mood.

450 to 500g (1lb) stewing veal, diced
4 generous tblsp EACH dried mushroom and onion flakes
1 can (400g or 14oz) plum tomatoes in tomato juice
1 tsp dried basil
1½ tsp salt
6 tblsp cold water
1 tblsp cornflour
6 tblsp Marsala

1 Put veal, mushrooms, onions, tomatoes and juice from can, basil, salt and water into a saucepan.

2 Bring to boil, stirring, then lower heat and cover.

3 Simmer gently for 1 hour. To thicken, mix cornflour smoothly with Marsala.

4 Stir into veal and bring back to the boil. Simmer 2 minutes and serve.

VEAL WITH PINEAPPLE, WALNUTS AND RUM

Serves 4 to 6

Quite a stunner and a surprise packet which for once gives veal well-deserved kudos. Serve with baby new potatoes, mange tout and new carrots sprinkled with fresh dill.

50g (2oz) gammon, all fat removed
450g (1lb) stewing veal, cubed
40g (1½oz) walnuts, lightly toasted under the grill
300ml (½pt) water
1 small to medium pineapple
1 tsp salt
1 tsp Dijon mustard
175g (6oz) leek
1 tblsp cornflour
4 tblsp dark rum

1 Chop gammon, transfer to a saucepan and dry-fry until it begins to colour. Keep heat lowish to prevent burning.

2 Add veal to pan and also dry-fry until outside of cubes turn a white colour and lose their raw look.

3 Add walnuts and water then cook gently for 5 minutes.

4 Peel and cube pineapple. Add to pan with salt and mustard. Bring to boil, lower heat and cover. Simmer gently for 40 minutes.

5 Trim leek, wash thoroughly and finely shred. Add to veal and cook a further 20 minutes, covered.

6 To thicken, mix cornflour smoothly with rum. Add to pan and bring back to boil, stirring. Simmer a further 3 minutes.

VENISON AND TURKEY LOAF

Serves 6

Hot or cold, the loaf is mouth-watering and freezes to perfection. We love it at home, freshly baked with onion and whisky sauce (page 144), mashed potatoes, cranberry sauce and grilled mushrooms; cold in sandwiches with salad and a light touch of chutney.

75g (3oz) onions
350g (12oz) boned shoulder of venison
225g (8oz) boneless turkey breast
1 tblsp tomato purée
75g (3oz) fresh brown breadcrumbs
1 egg white from Grade 1 egg
1 tsp salt
¼ tsp dried thyme

1 Set oven to 180°C (350°F), Gas 4.

2 Line an oven tray with non-stick baking paper. Quarter onions. Cube venison and turkey. Mince all three together.

3 Put into bowl and thoroughly work in rest of ingredients.

4 With damp hands, transfer mixture to lined tray and shape into a loaf measuring about 18 by 10 by 4cm (7 by 4 by 1½ inches).

5 Bake 1 hour and serve as suggested above.

VENISON CASSEROLE WITH ASSORTED VEGETABLES AND OATMEAL

Serves 4 to 6

No attention required with this all-in-one braise which requires nothing other than some crusty rolls or pieces of French bread by way of accompaniments.

125g (4oz) parsnips
175g (6oz) carrots
225g (8oz) potatoes
225g (8oz) onions
125g (4oz) celery
175g (6oz) tomatoes
450 to 475g (1lb) boned shoulder of venison
2 tsp salt
2 tblsp coarse oatmeal
150ml (¼pt) hot water
chopped parsley

1 Set oven to 190°C (375°F), Gas 5.

2 Cut parsnips, carrots and potatoes into small cubes. Put into a 1·75 litre (3 pint) casserole.

3 Chop onions. Cut celery into thin diagonal slices. Chop tomatoes. Add to casserole.

4 Cube venison and mix in with salt, oatmeal and water. Stir well to mix then cover securely with a matching lid or foil.

5 Cook 1¾ to 2 hours. Spoon out on to warm plates and sprinkle each portion thickly with parsley.

VENISON BRAISE WITH RED CABBAGE

Serves 4 to 6

If you're into the sort of spicy red cabbage eaten in Scandinavia, you'll go for this in a big way. It is tantalisingly sweet-sour and the venison fits in with it as though they were made for each other. Eat with freshly boiled potatoes or celeriac.

125g (4oz) onions
500 to 525g (1¼lb) red cabbage
300ml (½pt) hot water
8 juniper berries
1 clove
3 heaped tblsp brown sweet pickle
1½ tsp salt
450 to 475g (1lb) boned venison shoulder, cubed

1 Finely shred onions and cabbage either in a food processor or by hand.

2 Transfer to a large saucepan and add water, juniper berries, clove, sweet pickle and salt.

3 Bring to boil, stirring. Lower heat and cover then simmer gently for 30 minutes.

4 Stir in venison and continue to simmer for 1¼ to 1½ hours until meat is tender and cooked through.

POULTRY

FRUITED POULTRY AND NUT SALAD

Serves 4

Interesting this and another useful way of using up leftover poultry. Eat with hot toast.

225g (8oz) cold cooked poultry – chicken, turkey, pheasant
white part of small leek
50g (2oz) radishes
125g (4oz) peeled and diced fresh orange
1 slice brown toast, cubed
8 to 9 tblsp Light Salad Dressing (page 146)
radicchio leaves
watercress or 8 lightly cooked mange tout

1 Cut chicken into small cubes and put into a mixing bowl.

2 Shred leek finely. Trim and thinly slice radishes. Add both to the poultry.

3 Mix in orange, toast and dressing then toss gently to mix.

4 Arrange on plates, the centres lined with radicchio leaves. Garnish with sprigs of watercress or mange tout. Eat soon to prevent toast cubes becoming soggy.

CHICKEN SALAD WITH TOFU AND TERIYAKI DRESSING

Serves 3 to 4

A salad mix with a familiar waft of oriental aromas. Eat with wedges of brown bread or rolls.

142g (5oz) tofu, drained
125g (4oz) cooked smoked chicken slices
(from delicatessens and some supermarkets)
225g (8oz) cherry tomatoes
1 smallish green-skinned apple
125g (4oz) celery
2 knobs preserved ginger in syrup
1 tblsp teriyaki sauce (Japanese, sold in bottles)
2 tblsp red wine raspberry vinegar
1 garlic clove, peeled and crushed
lettuce leaves

1 Cut tofu into small cubes and put into a bowl. Cut chicken into strips and add.

2 Halve tomatoes. Leave apple unpeeled then quarter, core and dice flesh into same-sized pieces as the tofu. Cut celery diagonally into thin strips and coarsely chop ginger. Add all to bowl.

3 Beat teriyaki sauce with vinegar and garlic. Add to salad and gently stir round.

4 Cover and leave to stand at kitchen temperature for about 2 hours so that flavours have time to meld together.

5 To serve, spoon into little bowls lined with lettuce.

SHORT-CUT CORONATION CHICKEN

Serves 4 to 6

Once the darling of the buffet party set, Coronation Chicken is less seen than it used to be, probably because of its lengthy preparation. Hopefully my own fast version will bring about a much deserved revival in all its low cholesterol glory.

4 heaped tblsp mango chutney, minus big pieces of fruit
2 rounded tsp tomato purée
2 tsp medium curry powder
350g (12oz) fromage frais
2 tsp lemon juice
450 to 500g (about 1lb) cold and cooked chicken, cut into smallish pieces

1 Put chutney into a saucepan with tomato purée and curry powder. Very slowly bring to boil and bubble gently for about 2 minutes.

2 Cool to lukewarm. Stir in fromage frais and lemon juice.

3 Fold in chicken, transfer to bowl, cover then refrigerate until cold.

4 Arrange on a lettuce-lined dish and serve with a rice or pasta salad. Also a green one, snappily dressed.

CHICKEN DHANSAK

Serves 4

*A Parsee style dish packed with Eastern spices and only very slightly hot.
It contains healthy lentils, fresh tomatoes and potatoes and goes
particularly well with Indian bread.*

1 garlic clove
175g (6oz) onions
2 tsp oil
1 tsp powdered cumin
2 tsp tumeric
½ tsp ground ginger
3 tsp medium strength curry powder
2 level tsp salt
400g (14oz) blanched and skinned tomatoes
275g (10oz) orange lentils
275g (10oz) potatoes
750ml (1¼pt) boiling water
2 tblsp tomato purée
4 medium sized chicken joints, skinned

1 Peel and crush garlic. Peel and chop onions.

2 Heat oil in a fairly large pan until sizzling then add garlic and onions.
Fry over medium heat until they just begin to turn gold.

3 Stir in next three spices, curry powder and salt.

4 Chop tomatoes and add to pan with the lentils. Leave over a low heat.

5 Peel and grate potatoes. Stir into lentil mixture with water and tomato
purée. Bring to the boil.

6 Wash and dry chicken. Remove skin, add to pan and cover. Simmer
gently for 1 hour.

MISSISSIPPI MICROWAVE CHICKEN

Serves 4

*Marvellous if you've just dashed in from a heavy day and need a fairly
fast meal with a bit of style to it. Try it with millet
and a fresh green salad.*

4 large boned chicken breasts, each 225g (8oz)
350g (12oz) tomatoes
175g (6oz) EACH:
green pepper
onions
celery

1 tsp salt

1 Skin chicken portions and arrange in a dish measuring 28cm (11 inch) in diameter by 5cm (2 inch) in depth.

2 Cover with cling film, nick twice and cook for 15 minutes at full power in a 650 watt microwave oven.

3 Meanwhile chop tomatoes, de-seeded pepper, onions and celery.

4 Pour chicken liquid out of dish as it may be fatty. Top chicken with prepared vegetables and sprinkle with salt.

5 Cover as above and cook a further 25 minutes. Stand 5 minutes before serving.

HONOURABLE CHICKEN WINGS IN SOY SAUCE

Serves 4

A typical Westernised stir-fry with ginger, mushrooms and spring onions. Accompany with freshly cooked Chinese noodles and a dessert of canned lychees or mandarins. It's a fairly economical main course and quick to make.

6 spring onions
2 tsp oil
12 plump chicken wings
175ml (6 fluid oz) water
150g (6oz) mushrooms
3 knobs preserved ginger in syrup
2 tsp cornflour
1 tblsp soy sauce
1 tblsp medium sherry
1 tblsp ginger syrup
½ tsp salt

1 Trim and chop onions. Heat oil in a frying pan or wok then add onions and wings.

2 Fry quickly until lightly browned. Pour in water, bring to boil and cover. Simmer gently for 20 minutes.

3 Trim mushrooms and cut into thin slices. Thinly slice ginger. Add both to chicken then cover and simmer for a further 12 minutes.

4 Blend cornflour smoothly with soy sauce, sherry, ginger syrup and salt.

5 Pour over wings, stir in well and bubble gently for 3 to 4 minutes until liquid thickens.

TANDOORI CHICKEN

Serves 8

No tandoor clay oven, so what of tandoori chicken? Fortunately it works almost as well in a conventional oven and with the help of some shop bought spice mix, I turned out a great replica which eight of us, all curry buffs, tucked into with enthusiasm and appreciation.

1 by 2¾kg (6lb) chicken
225g (8oz) set yogurt
2 tblsp tandoori spice mix
1 tsp EACH:
turmeric
cumin
salt
1 tblsp lemon juice
lettuce leaves and tomato slices for serving
wedges of lemon

1 Set oven to 180°C (350°F), Gas 4.

2 Skin chicken completely except for wings which resist all efforts. Slash flesh all over with a sharp knife at 2·5cm (1inch) intervals. Make cuts fairly deep. Stand bird on a grid in a fairly large roasting tin.

3 Mix yogurt with tandoori spice mix, turmeric, cumin, salt and lemon juice.

4 Spread thickly over chicken, getting the paste right into the slashed flesh.

5 Cover loosely with foil and refrigerate about 8 to 10 hours.

6 Uncover and roast 1½ hours or until chicken looks charred.

7 Carve as you would normally and stand slices on plates lined with lettuce and tomato wedges. Add 1 or 2 wedges of lemon to each portion.

CHICKEN IN RATATOUILLE

Serves 4

A dish that flows with Mediterranean warmth. So delicious and no trouble. Eat with plain boiled rice.

4 chicken joints, each about 225 to 350g (8 to 12oz)
2 cans (each 400g or 14oz) chopped tomatoes
225g (8oz) courgettes
225g (8oz) onions
225g (8oz) aubergines
1½ tsp salt
1 tsp herbes de Provence

1 Skin joints then wash and dry. Put into a fairly large saucepan with the chopped tomatoes. Leave uncovered and slowly bring to boil.

2 Thinly slice courgettes and onions. Cut aubergine into small cubes.

3 Add to pan with salt. Bring to boil, stirring. Cover and simmer 1 to 1¼ hours or until chicken is tender. Stir from time to time to prevent sticking. Finally mix in dried herbs.

HUNGARIAN CHICKEN WITH CARAWAY

Serves 4

A relic from the Austro-Hungarian Empire but especially toned down for the book by excluding lard, Hungary's premier choice of fat for sweet and savoury dishes. But no harm done by the omission, as you will see. Serve in traditional style with boiled potatoes.

175g (6oz) onions
2 medium peppers in green and yellow, each 125 to 150g (4 to 5oz)
2 tsp oil
500g (1 to 1¼lb) ripe and bright red tomatoes, blanched and skinned
1¼kg (2lb) chicken drumsticks
1 tsp caraway seeds
4 tsp paprika (sweet red pepper in powder form)
1 tsp salt
1 garlic clove, peeled and crushed
1 tsp sugar

1 Grate onions on coarse side of grater or finely chop. Halve and de-seed peppers then cut flesh into fine strips.

2 Heat oil in a saucepan. Add prepared vegetables and fry gently until just beginning to turn creamy gold.

3 Chop tomatoes. Remove skin from drumsticks and discard. Add chicken to pan with all remaining ingredients.

4 Bring to boil, stirring. Lower heat and cover. Simmer 45 to 55 minutes until chicken is tender. If preferred, use chicken thighs instead of the drumsticks.

CHICKEN PAPRIKÁS WITH YOGURT

Serves 4

Skilfully in the Hungarian mould, this classic dish should be eaten with pasta shells and delicate green vegetables – French beans, mange tout or courgettes, cut into spears and lightly cooked.

4 portions of chicken, each about 225g (8oz)
225g (8oz) green peppers
225g (8oz) onions
3 tblsp tomato purée
1½ tsp salt
1 bay leaf
150ml (¼pt) boiling water
225g (8oz) yogurt

1 Skin chicken and put into a large saucepan.

2 De-seed and chop peppers. Cut onions into thin slices. Add to pan with all remaining ingredients except yogurt.

3 Bring to boil, stirring. Lower heat and cover. Simmer 1 to 1¼ hours until chicken is cooked through.

4 Stir fairly often as tomato mixtures have a habit of sticking if cooked for any length of time.

5 Stir in yogurt and warm mixture through without boiling.

CHICKEN WITH BAKED BEANS, LEEKS AND MUSHROOMS

Serves 4

An easy option for busy people, the mix of ingredients puts this whole thing into top class cooking – one of those lucky breaks that happens every so often when mixing fresh and canned produce. Eat with carrots, sprouts and mashed potatoes.

4 portions of chicken, each about 225g (8oz)
1 can (447g or 15½oz) baked beans in tomato sauce
2 medium leeks
125g (4oz) button mushrooms
300ml (½pt) water
1 to 1½ tsp salt

1 Skin chicken and put into a large pan with beans.

2 Trim leeks and thoroughly wash. Repeat with mushrooms. Slice leeks but leave mushrooms whole. Add to pan.

3 Pour in water and salt. Bring to boil, stirring gently. Lower heat and cover.

4 Simmer gently about 1¼ hours until chicken is cooked through.

CHICKEN SAAG GOSHT

Serves 4

*Preferable to restaurant versions because of its low fat content, I have
exchanged chicken for lamb and the result is a fairly honest reproduction
of an Indian dish, tastefully spiced and only mildly hot. Eat with Indian
bread and Raita (page 139) plus a cool side salad of diced up tomatoes,
cucumber and onion, all sprinkled with fresh lime juice.*

150g (5oz) onions
2 tsp oil
1 garlic clove, peeled and crushed
3 tsp medium curry powder
1½ tsp ginger
2 tsp cumin
1 tsp paprika
1 tsp turmeric
1½ tsp salt
8 boneless and skinless chicken thighs
450 to 500g (1lb) frozen spinach
225g (8oz) yogurt

1 Finely chop onions. Sizzle oil in a fairly large saucepan. Add onions and
garlic and fry gently until they both turn pale gold.

2 Add curry powder, ginger, cumin, paprika, turmeric and salt. Continue to
fry gently for 3 minutes, stirring twice or three times.

3 Add chicken, spinach and yogurt. Bring to boil, lower heat and cover.
Cook slowly for 1 hour until chicken is really tender.

4 Uncover and continue to cook slowly, stirring occasionally, for a further
15 to 20 minutes to evaporate some of the liquid.

CREAMY RAISIN CHICKEN WITH BANANA ON CRUMPETS

Serves 4 to 6

A completely off-beat contribution which is distinctively mild and suitable for lunch or a snacky supper. Using crumpets as a base is an 'invention' of mine and has worked out better than I'd hoped.

675 to 700g (1¼lb) cooked chicken
2 tblsp cornflour
300ml (½pt) milk
1 large banana
50g (2oz) raisins
½ tsp salt
1 tblsp lemon juice
4 to 6 freshly toasted crumpets
paprika

1 Cut chicken into small dice.

2 Tip cornflour into a saucepan. Mix smoothly with a little milk. Add remainder.

3 Cook, stirring, until sauce comes to the boil and thickens. Simmer 1 minute. Add chicken and heat through for 10 minutes.

4 Slice in banana then fold in raisins, salt and lemon juice. Simmer 2 minutes.

5 Arrange crumpets on warm plate and top each with chicken mixture. Sprinkle lightly with paprika.

INDOOR BARBECUE CHICKEN WITH CIDER BASTE

Serves 4

A memorable affair and highly recommended for a small and intimate dinner party. Serve the baby chickens with a selection of seasonal cooked vegetables or with a leafy salad made from mixed lettuce.

4 poussin, each about 450 to 500g (1lb)
150ml (¼pt) cider
1 tblsp Worcestershire sauce
2 tblsp tomato ketchup
2 tblsp pineapple or apricot jam
2 tsp coarse grained mustard with whisky or on its own

1 Wash and dry poussin and transfer to a large roasting tin. Set oven to 190°C (375°F), Gas 5.

2 For barbecue style baste, pour cider into a pan. Add all remaining ingredients then bring to boil, stirring.

3 Lower heat, leave uncovered and continue to boil gently for 9 to 10 minutes.

4 Pour equal amounts over poussin and roast 1 hour, basting twice.

CHILI CON POLLO, VERSION 1

Serves 4

Dressed-up with chicken instead of beef.

450 to 500g (1lb or just over) of boned chicken breasts
1 tsp oil
1 garlic clove, peeled and crushed
450 to 500g (1lb) ripe tomatoes
1 tsp paprika
2 tsp mild seasoned chili powder (almost brown in colour)
1 tsp salt
2 to 3 pinches cayenne pepper to increase heat
1 tsp Worcestershire sauce
2 tblsp tomato purée
1 can (400g or 14oz) red kidney beans, drained
1 tblsp cornflour
3 tblsp cold water

1 Skin and coarsely mince chicken and put into a saucepan with oil.

2 Add garlic and fry over medium heat, stirring occasionally, until chicken loses its raw look and begins to turn brown.

3 Meanwhile, blanch and skin tomatoes and chop. Add to pan with paprika, chili powder, salt, cayenne pepper, Worcestershire sauce and purée.

4 Bring to boil, stirring. Lower heat and cover then simmer for 45 minutes. Add beans.

5 Blend cornflour smoothly with water, add to chili and bubble, stirring gently, until thickened. Simmer 6 minutes. Serve piping hot with rice.

CHILI CON POLLO, VERSION 2

Serves 4

Unusually thickened with oat bran, this chili is less like the traditional one we're used to but the addition of wine lends its own touch of character and the whole thing is appealingly edible.

3 medium leeks
300ml (½pt) dry red wine
500g (1lb) boned and skinned chicken breasts
1kg (2lb) tomatoes, blanched, skinned, chopped
1½ tsp salt
4 tblsp tomato purée
25g (1oz) oat bran
2 tsp mild seasoned chili powder
1 tsp paprika
2 or 3 shakes Tabasco sauce
1 can (400g or 1lb) red kidney beans, drained

1 Trim and very finely shred leeks, leaving on only a small amount of the green parts. Put into a pan with the wine.

2 Leave uncovered. Cook slowly, stirring periodically, until most of the wine has evaporated and leeks begin to turn pink.

3 Mix in all remaining ingredients except beans. Bring gently to boil, stirring.

4 Lower heat and cover then simmer for 40 minutes. Add beans and heat through for about 5 minutes. Serve with rice or millet.

KUMQUAT CHICKEN WITH BRANDY AND PEPPERS

Serves 6

*A magical marriage and a memorable main course, richly-coloured and
tenderly flavoured. Serve with millet or bulgar and salad of
sliced button mushrooms, chopped onions and cress, all tossed in
fresh strained orange juice.*

6 large and partially-boned chicken breasts, each 225g (8oz)
juice of 2 medium oranges
5 tblsp water
1 garlic clove, peeled and crushed
½ tsp mixed spice
1 tsp salt
4 tblsp brandy
10 kumquats
1 medium red pepper
15g (½oz) fresh coriander, chopped

1 Skin chicken breasts then wash and dry. Arrange, in single layer, in
large frying pan.

2 Combine orange juice with water, garlic, spice, salt and brandy. Pour
over chicken.

3 Wash and dry kumquats, halve lengthwise and remove pips. De-seed
pepper and cut into narrow strips.

4 Arrange both on top of chicken with half the coriander. Bring to the boil,
lower heat and cover. Simmer gently for 1 hour. Sprinkle each portion with
rest of coriander.

RED ONION CHICKEN WITH WINE AND SWEETCORN

Serves 4

Deceptively sophisticated. Eat with toasted muffins and small bowls of grated carrots and raisins tossed with lemon juice.

4 portions of chicken, each about 225g (8oz)
1 can (411g or 14½oz) cream style corn
75g (3oz) red onions
150g (5oz) bulb of fennel
300ml (½pt) dry red wine
2 tblsp tomato purée
1½ tsp salt

1 Skin chicken and put into a large saucepan. Add corn.

2 Slice onions. Cut trimmed fennel into narrow strips. Sprinkle both over chicken.

3 Whisk wine, purée and salt together until well-blended. Pour into pan, bring to the boil then lower heat and cover.

4 Simmer 1 to 1¼ hours until chicken is cooked through, stirring from time to time.

APRICOT AND TURKEY KEBABS WITH MUSTARD BASTE

Serves 4

Expect the apricots to take on a charred look – it's part and parcel of these sweet-sour, fruity kebabs which I serve on a bed of millet or mixture of white and wild rice. Make a large mixed salad of your choice to go with them.

125g (4oz) dried apricots
hot water
450 to 500g (1lb) boned turkey breast
3 tsp Dijon mustard
2 tblsp lemon juice
1½ tsp oil

1 Soak apricots in water to cover for 30 minutes. Drain thoroughly.

2 Cube turkey and thread on to 4 skewers, each 20cm (8 inch) long, alternately with apricots.

3 Beat together mustard, lemon juice and oil.

4 Line grill pan with foil. Put in the kebabs and brush with baste. Grill a total of 15 minutes, turning 4 times and brushing with remaining baste.

PINEAPPLE AND TURKEY KEBABS WITH APPLE BASTE

Serves 4

*Make as Apricot and Turkey Kebabs (page 104) but omit the apricots.
Thread turkey on to 4 skewers with half a medium-sized fresh cubed
pineapple and 75g (3oz) button mushrooms, stalks removed. Prepare baste
from 2 tblsp apple juice beaten with 1 tblsp clear honey, 1 tblsp
Worcestershire sauce, 1 tblsp wine vinegar, 2 tsp oil and 1 tsp salt.*

TURKEY BRAISE WITH RED PLUMS

Serves 4

Turkey in Sunday best. Accompany with a bowl of mashed potatoes browned in the oven and any greens in season – or cauliflower.

225g (8oz) EACH:
courgettes
celery
onions
carrots
parsnips
cauliflower florets

300ml (½pt) boiling water
2 tblsp redcurrant jelly
4 tsp coarse grained mustard
2 tsp salt
8 boneless turkey thighs
350g (12oz) black or red plums

1 Set oven to 200°C (400°F), Gas 6.

2 Wash and trim vegetables, peel where necessary and cut all of them into thin slices. Spread over base of large casserole.

3 Combine water with jelly, mustard and salt. Stir until jelly melts then pour half over vegetables. Arrange turkey thighs on top and coat with rest of liquid.

4 Halve plums and remove stones. Arrange, cut sides down, on top of turkey.

5 Cover dish with lid or foil and cook for 2 hours.

COUNTRIFIED TURKEY STEWPOT WITH FENNEL AND HERBS

Serves 4

My note to myself when I tasted the stew for the first time: "Marvellous, subtle flavour. Attractively green from the herbs. Worth including." And so it is but do ensure you use fresh herbs only. Serve with boiled new potatoes or a bowl of mash.

125g (4oz) onions
2 tsp oil
1 large bulb of fennel
450 to 500g (1lb) diced turkey breast
325ml (approximately 9 fluid oz) lager
1 tsp salt
1 tblsp cornflour
4 tblsp cold water
2 tsp EACH:
chopped fennel fronds
thyme
marjoram
tarragon
parsley
chives

1 Chop onions finely. Sizzle oil in saucepan, add onions and fry gently for about 10 minutes until they just begin to turn golden.

2 Thinly slice fennel with a sharp, strong knife. Add to pan with the turkey, lager and salt.

3 Bring to boil, cover and simmer for 40 minutes until turkey is cooked.

4 To thicken, blend cornflour smoothly with the cold water. Add to pan. Cook, stirring, until mixture comes to the boil and thickens.

5 Simmer for 2 minutes then stir in the herbs.

TURKEY STUFFED AUBERGINES WITH TOMATOES AND MUSHROOMS

Serves 4

A true friend with Middle East overtones and always worth eating. Also filling with new potatoes.

2 aubergines, each about 275g (10oz)
50g (2oz) onions
1 garlic clove, peeled and chopped
2 tsp oil
225g (8oz) raw minced turkey breast
150g (5oz) blanched and skinned tomatoes
75g (3oz) mushrooms
40g (1½oz) fresh white breadcrumbs
½ to 1 tsp salt
¼ tsp cinnamon

1 Set oven to 180°C (350°F), Gas 4. Lightly oil a flattish baking tray.

2 Wash and dry aubergines them make a cut line, lengthwise, all the way round to stop the skins from bursting.

3 Bake 45 minutes. Meanwhile, grate onion and put into a saucepan with the garlic and oil. Fry gently until the onions soften and begin to turn gold.

4 Mix in turkey and cook a little more briskly, still stirring, until meat is crumbly. Remove from heat.

5 Chop tomatoes and mushrooms. Mix into turkey mixture with last three ingredients.

6 Take aubergines out of the oven and halve each round the cut line with a sharp knife.

7 Scoop out middles (taking care not to puncture the skins) then chop flesh finely. Add to turkey filling and mix thoroughly.

8 Return aubergine shells to tray and pack with filling. Reheat for 25 minutes.

TURKEY, MUSHROOM AND WINE SAUCE FOR FRESH PASTA

Serves 3 to 4

A light and appealing pasta sauce made with turkey breast. For colour contrast, serve with green noodles.

2 tsp oil
1 garlic clove, peeled and crushed
350g (12oz) raw turkey breast, skinned and minced
300ml (½pt) rosé wine
½ to 1 level tsp salt
1 tblsp cornflour
3 tblsp water
200g (7oz) button mushrooms
3 large pinches of nutmeg

1 Sizzle oil in a saucepan. Add garlic and turkey.

2 Fry 7 to 10 minutes over medium heat until turkey loses its raw look and starts to brown. Stir frequently.

3 Pour in wine and add salt. Cover and simmer 10 minutes.

4 Mix cornflour smoothly with water. Slice mushrooms. Add both to turkey mixture with nutmeg.

5 Bubble until thickened, stirring. Simmer gently a further 5 minutes.

WINE-BRAISED PHEASANT WITH PRUNES AND MUSTARD

Serves 8

Pheasants (low cholesterol) are now on sale when in season from leading supermarket chains and speciality butchers, making availability for those living in towns and cities, without recourse to country shoots, considerably easier than it used to be. With superior-tasting lean meat, and not much more expensive than top quality poultry, use pheasants to make this festive-tasting winter main course with its superb, deep brown sauce and exquisite aroma. Once degreased, and I'll explain how to do this later, fat will be minimal and you can indulge with an easy conscience. Plain boiled potatoes go down well, as does caraway cabbage (page 140) and cranberry sauce.

1 brace of pheasant (2 birds), weighing about 1½kg (3lb) between them
3 generous tsp Dijon mustard
1 tsp salt
450ml (¾pt) red wine
1 tblsp redcurrant jelly, melted
1 tblsp Worcestershire sauce
175g (6oz) pitted prunes
1 tblsp cornflour
150ml (¼pt) cold water

1 Skin pheasants (except for wings which are difficult) then remove as much fat as possible. Also take out shot.

2 Divide each bird into 4 portions and dry-fry in a large, non-stick pan until pieces are well browned. Turn often and keep heat under pan moderate.

3 Mix together mustard, salt, wine, jelly and Worcestershire sauce. Pour over pheasant then scatter prunes over the top. Bring to boil, lower heat and cover. Simmer gently for 50 minutes to 1 hour or until meat is tender.

4 Transfer pheasant portions into one dish, gravy into another. Cover both and when cold, refrigerate for about 8 hours.

5 Before serving, skim off fat from top of gravy and discard. Pour gravy into a clean pan and bring to a gentle boil. Stir in cornflour mixed smoothly with cold water. Bubble until thickened.

6 Add pheasant, cover and re-boil for 25 to 30 minutes or until well heated through.

VEGETARIAN

THREE MUSHROOM STIR-FRY WITH TOFU AND SPRING ONIONS

Serves 3 to 4

A slightly oriental stir-fry, quickly made, which has a subtle and lingering taste. Team it with Chinese noodles and some extra chili and soy sauces for those who want stronger flavours. The tofu makes it a balanced meal – no extra protein necessary.

125g (4oz) oyster mushrooms
125g (4oz) shii-taki mushrooms
50 to 75g (2 to 3oz) chanterelle mushrooms
5 large spring onions
1 tblsp oil
1 packet (284g or 10oz) tofu, drained
1 tblsp cornflour
2 tblsp ginger wine
1 tblsp soy sauce
5 tblsp water
1 tsp salt
¼ tsp chili sauce

1 Trim mushrooms, wash well, dry thoroughly then cut up into smallish pieces.

2 Trim onions and cut into thin slices from heads to green tails.

3 Sizzle oil in a wok or frying pan. Add onions and stir-fry fairly briskly for 1 minute. Add mushrooms and continue to stir-fry, but not quite as briskly, for 3½ minutes. Take off heat.

4 Cut tofu into small cubes. Mix cornflour smoothly with wine, soy sauce, water, salt and chili sauce.

5 Add tofu and cornflour mixture to mushrooms. Stir-fry fairly briskly until mixture bubbles and thickens – about 2 to 3 minutes. Serve straight away.

MIXED VEGETABLE STIR-FRY WITH TOFU AND COURGETTE

Serves 4

Similar to the Mixed Vegetable Stir-Fry with Fresh Salmon and walnuts on page 53, here is a completely vegetarian version. Substitute 285g or just over 10oz tofu for salmon, include 1 medium sliced courgette with all the other vegetables and use sherry instead of ginger wine. Cut tofu into small cubes then gently stir into ingredients in pan or wok just before adding the cornflour mixture.

VEGETABLE CURRY WITH CHICK-PEAS

Serves 6

A vegetarian bounty with a truly authentic Indian flavour. It owes its success to a Midlands restaurateur who kindly gave me his own blend of spices. Eat with Indian bread.

1 tblsp oil
1 tsp black mustard seeds
1 tsp turmeric
3 tsp garam masala
2 tsp cumin
seeds from 6 opened out green cardamon pods
4 cloves
¼ tsp cayenne pepper
1 garlic clove, peeled and crushed
175g (6oz) onions
350g (12oz) leek
225g (8oz) carrots
450g (1lb) celeriac or potatoes
225g (8oz) aubergines
275g (10oz) parsnip
600ml (1pt) boiling water
4 tblsp tomato purée
2 tsp salt
1 can (425g or 15oz) chick-peas

1 Heat oil in a large saucepan until sizzling. Add the next 7 ingredients (all the spices). Fry gently for 5 minutes then leave pan over a low heat.

2 Stir round and add garlic.

3 Thinly slice onions. Finely shred washed leek. Cut carrots into thin slices. Cut celeriac or potatoes into cubes. Repeat with unpeeled aubergines and peeled parsnip.

4 Add to pan and mix in well with the spices. Mix water with purée and salt. Pour over vegetables then bring to boil, stirring all the time.

5 Lower heat and cover. Simmer 45 minutes. Stir in chick-peas with liquid from can and continue to simmer fairly gently, covered, for about 20 minutes.

ALMOST INSTANT VEGETABLE CURRY

Serves 6

A quick-as-a-flash curry, based on cans for almost total convenience. The fat content is about 1·1gm per serving which is reasonable for ready-prepared products. Best with rice or warmed through Indian bread.

1 can (400g or 14oz) caponata (Italian mixed vegetables)
1 can (400g or 14oz) peperonata (peppers in tomato sauce)
2 tsp garam masala
2 tsp medium curry powder
1 tsp cumin
300ml (½pt) water
1 tsp salt
25g (1oz) coriander leaves

1 Tip canned vegetables into a saucepan with all remaining ingredients except coriander.

2 Bring to boil, lower heat and cover. Simmer 30 minutes, stirring from time to time.

3 Chop coriander and mix into curry. Stir round and serve.

PURELY VEGETARIAN STUFFED PEPPERS WITH MILLET

Serves 4

A compatible partnership this – peppers stuffed with vegetables and millet, simmered in tomato liquid and served hot or cold; whichever suits the occasion. They look like something dished up in southern Europe and a bit messy but what a flavour . . .

4 large red or green peppers
125g (4oz) EACH:
carrots
parsnip
celery
white part of leek
50g (2oz) turnip
50g (2oz) shallots
75g (3oz) millet
300ml (½pt) water
1 tsp salt
450ml (¾pt) hot water
4 tblsp tomato juice
2 tblsp lemon juice
1½ tsp salt

1 Wash and dry peppers. Cut a slice off the stalk end of each and reserve for lids. Remove inside fibres and seeds. If peppers tend to topple over when stood upright, cut thin slivers off bases to steady them.

2 Stand compactly together in a saucepan.

3 Finely chop or grate all vegetables either by hand or in a food processor.

4 Tip into a bowl and add millet, water and salt. Spoon into peppers, placing any leftover filling into pan. Top each with a lid.

118

5 To cook, combine water with rest of ingredients and pour into pan.

6 Bring to boil and cover. Simmer gently for 45 minutes when vegetables should be tender and millet puffed up. Eat hot or cold.

SPINACH AND MUSHROOM LASAGNE WITH COTTAGE CHEESE

Serves 6

Something to whet the appetites of vegetarians and carnivors alike, the preparation does take a bit of time so bear with it if you're interested.

225 to 250g (8 to 9oz) fresh or dry lasagne leaves
350g (12oz) frozen chopped spinach
225g (8oz) frozen petits champignons
3 tblsp water
2 tsp salt
2 tblsp cornflour
150ml (¼pt) milk
1 can (400g or 14oz) tomatoes in tomato juice
½ tsp nutmeg
350g (12oz) cottage cheese
2 tsp grated Parmesan cheese

1 Set oven to 220°C (425°F), Gas 7.

2 Cook lasagne as directed on the packet then drain thoroughly.

3 Put spinach, champignons, water and 1 tsp salt into a saucepan. Bring to boil, stirring all the time, to break down spinach. Leave uncovered and simmer 25 to 30 minutes to evaporate most of the liquid.

4 Tip cornflour into a second clean pan and blend smoothly with a little milk. Stir in remainder. Cook, stirring, until mixture forms a thickish sauce. Simmer 1 minute.

5 Mix tomatoes and juice from can into cornflour sauce. Break up tomatoes with a spoon then bring sauce to the boil, stirring frequently. Mix in nutmeg and rest of salt.

6 To assemble, fill a lightly oiled 23cm (9 inch) dish, depth of 6cm (2½ inch), with alternate layers of lasagne, spinach mixture, tomato sauce and cottage cheese.

7 Begin with pasta and end with cheese. Sprinkle with Parmesan then reheat and brown in oven for 25 minutes.

HOT BEETS WITH SPRING ONIONS, FENNEL AND CHIVES IN FROMAGE FRAIS

Serves 6

It's a pity not to take beetroots seriously as a hot vegetable. They are quite superb and team harmoniously with fish and poultry or, in their own right, as a main course with rice or millet. Also cooked in the microwave.

700g (1½lb) cooked beetroots
8 spring onions
1 tsp salt
125g (4oz) fromage frais
1 tblsp EACH: chopped chives and feathery fennel (the herb not the vegetable)

1 Peel beets and cut into narrow strips. Transfer to a 1·2 litre (2 pint) oven to table dish.

2 Trim onions and chop fairly finely. Stir into beetroots with salt.

3 Cover with cling film, slit twice and cook for 6 minutes at full power in a 650 watt microwave oven.

4 Uncover, gently mix in the fromage frais, wipe edges of dish clean and sprinkle with the herbs.

121

BRIGHT YELLOW AND ORANGE SPAGHETTI SAUCE

Serves 4 to 5

A vibrantly glowing sauce to have on hand for spaghetti; all vegetarian, deeply-flavoured and made with fleshy Dutch peppers. Topped with fromage frais and a dusting of Parmesan, you have chic upon chic, Italian style.

125g (4oz) onions
450 to 500g (1 to 1¼lb) mixed yellow and orange peppers
2 tsp oil
300ml (½pt) vegetable stock (the real thing or made with cube and water)
1 tsp salt
½ tsp dried basil or 1 tblsp finely chopped fresh
about 250g (8oz) fromage frais
4 to 5 tsp grated Parmesan cheese

1 Peel and chop onions. Wash and dry peppers then halve and de-seed. Coarsely chop flesh.

2 Sizzle oil in a pan. Add onions and fry gently until just beginning to turn gold.

3 Stir in peppers and stock. Bring to the boil, lower heat and cover. Simmer gently for 45 minutes.

4 Blend, with liquid, to smooth purée in blender goblet.

5 Return to pan, add salt and basil and reheat until hot, stirring.

6 Serve on brown spaghetti, allowing 75g (3oz) raw weight per person.

7 Top each portion with fromage frais and a sprinkling of the Parmesan.

WATERCRESS AND TOMATO STUFFED MUSHROOMS WITH WHITE WINE

Serves 4

Using those giant mushrooms one comes across from time to time, these are a great all-vegetarian side dish, just the thing to go with cottage or half fat Cheddar cheese for a midday or evening meal. Eat with crusty seeded rolls.

4 very large open mushrooms, each 75 to 125g (3 to 4oz)
75g (3oz) onions
50ml (2 fluid oz) white wine
75g (3oz) watercress
150g (5oz) brown bread
225g (8oz) tomatoes
2 tsp oil
1 tblsp Worcestershire sauce
¼ to ½ tsp salt

1 Set oven to 200°C (400°F), Gas 6.

2 Wash mushrooms and dry with paper towels. Remove stalks and chop.

3 Chop onions finely and put into saucepan with the wine. Bring to a gentle boil, leave uncovered and simmer until all the liquid has evaporated.

4 Chop watercress finely. Convert bread into crumbs. Blanch, skin and chop tomatoes. Add all three to onions in pan then mix in stalks, oil, Worcestershire sauce and salt.

5 Spoon on top of mushrooms and put into a baking dish lightly brushed with oil.

6 Reheat for 20 minutes.

POTATO SALAD WITH ONIONS

Serves 4 to 6

Just the thing to go with cold poultry and fish in the summer.

450 to 500g (1lb) boiled potatoes
8 large spring onions
8 tblsp Light Salad Dressing (page 146)

1 Cube potatoes and put into large mixing bowl.

2 Trim onions and chop. Add to potatoes with dressing.

3 Toss gently to mix. Serve at room temperature.

MIXED BEAN SALAD WITH CARROT DRESSING

Serves 6 to 8

Perfect for a buffet, the bean salad can also be converted into a nutritious main course with any kind of grain – millet, rice, buckwheat, bulgar. The carrot juice dressing is different from the usual run and the salad is fast to make with canned beans.

1 can (425 to 450g or 15oz) EACH:
haricot beans
flageolet beans
black eyed beans

150ml (¼pt) carrot juice
1 or 2 garlic cloves, peeled and crushed
2 tblsp white wine vinegar
3 tsp salad oil
1 tsp salt
2 heaped tblsp chopped parsley

1 Drain and thoroughly rinse beans in a colander then leave to drain, covered, until dry.

2 Tip into a large mixing bowl and toss over and over until thoroughly mixed.

3 Beat carrot juice with garlic, vinegar, oil and salt.

4 Pour over beans, toss well to mix then transfer to a salad bowl. Sprinkle thickly with parsley before serving.

SALADS
AND
SIDE DISHES

BULGAR

With minimal fat and packed with fibre, bulgar (also called burghul or cracked wheat) is basically wholewheat grain which has been partially cooked, dried and cracked, making the finishing-off a quick and trouble-free operation. A staple in the Middle East, bulgar can be served cold as a salad or hot in place of rice, pasta or potatoes. Two schools of thought seem to govern its preparation. Some soak the bulgar for a given length of time then drain and use it. Others cook it briefly. Both methods work well, leaving the grain firm in taste and texture.

SOAKED BULGAR

225g (8oz) bulgar
900ml (1½pt) boiling water
1 tsp salt

1 Put bulgar into a bowl. Stir in water and salt.

2 Leave 10 minutes then drain.

COOKED BULGAR

225g (8oz) bulgar
900ml (1½pt) boiling water
1 tsp salt

1 Tip bulgar into a saucepan. Add water and salt then stir round with a fork.

2 Bring back to boil and simmer for 5 minutes, keeping pan covered.

3 Uncover and continue to simmer a further 2 to 3 minutes. Drain.

BULGAR SALAD IN WALDORF STYLE

A variation on one of North America's popular salads. Eat with poultry or fish.

125g (4oz) soaked or cooked bulgar
75g (3oz) celery
50g (2oz) walnuts
6 medium spring onions
½ tsp salt
2 tblsp low calorie dressing

1 Tip bulgar into a bowl.

2 Finely chop celery and walnuts. Mix into bulgar.

3 Trim and chop spring onions then add with salt and dressing.

MINTED BULGAR SALAD IN MIDDLE EAST STYLE

Serves 6

Designed to go with low fat cheeses and fish such as mackerel and herrings. In its countries of origin, the salad is more likely to be called Taboulleh.

225g (8oz) soaked or cooked bulgar
1 garlic clove, peeled and crushed
3 tblsp finely chopped fresh mint or 2 tsp concentrated mint sauce
2 tblsp lemon juice
2 tsp oil
salt and pepper to taste

1 Tip bulgar into a mixing bowl.

2 Fork in garlic, mint, lemon juice and oil.

3 Season to taste with salt and pepper.

PILAF SALAD WITH RAISINS AND PIMIENTOS

Serves 6

A bright spark here, the salad is friendly towards roast poultry or turkey kebabs (page 104-5) and also stands up well as a dish in its own right with a salad of lettuce tossed with low calorie dressing, one of mine or shop bought. If you can, use three different types of lettuce for colour contrast, choosing from cos, webb, oakleaf, Chinese leaves and radicchio (red chicory).

225g (8oz) soaked or cooked bulgar, drained
75g (3oz) raisins
2 tsp olive oil
1 garlic clove, peeled and crushed
150g (5oz) cottage cheese
1 can (400g or 14oz) sweet red peppers (pimientos) in brine
1 tblsp lemon juice
1 teacup chopped parsley

1 Tip bulgar into a mixing bowl.

2 Fork in raisins, oil, garlic and cheese.

3 Drain, rinse and chop peppers (not too small). Add to bulgar with lemon juice.

4 Toss gently to mix, transfer to a glass serving dish (for the colours to show through) and cover top thickly with parsley.

FANCY TABOULLEH

Serves 6

Make as previous recipe but stir in half a small diced cucumber and 225g (8oz) halved cherry tomatoes. Arrange in a lettuce-lined bowl and sprinkle lightly with parsley. Stud sparingly with black olives then garnish with thin strips of green pepper.

LEBANESE TABOULLEH

Serves 6

From the Middle Eastern Yeldizlar restaurant in London comes this heavily-herbed salad which was served to us as part of the open table (the meze). The owner kindly explained how it was made and this is my interpretation of the original.

125g (4oz) soaked or cooked bulgar
40g (1½oz) parsley
25g (1oz) onion
2 tsp oil
2 tsp lemon juice
2 tsp concentrated bottled mint in vinegar
75g (3oz) chopped tomatoes

1 Tip bulgar into a bowl.

2 Finely chop parsley and grate onion. Fork into bulgar with oil, lemon juice, mint and tomatoes.

CHESTNUTS WITH BROWN RICE

Serves 8

Different from run-of-the-mill side dishes, this curious combination of cooked dried chestnuts, slightly smoky-flavoured, and brown rice is ideal with chicken and turkey. Useful at Christmas.

225g (8oz) dried chestnuts
600ml (1pt) cold water
225g (8oz) brown rice
boiling water
1½ tsp salt

1 Soak chestnuts overnight in plenty of cold water so that they return to their usual size. Drain and cook in the cold water for 1 to 1½ hours until very tender.

2 Halfway through, cook brown rice as directed on the packet in the boiling water and salt.

3 Drain chestnuts, rinse under cold water then break into small pieces. Drain rice if necessary, return to pan and stand over a low heat.

4 Mix in chestnuts with a fork, cover and reheat slowly on the hob. Alternatively, do this in the microwave for a few minutes or in a warm oven for about 20 minutes.

BARLEY

Serves 8

A low cholesterol side dish which is sadly under used, despite its economy price tag. Serve instead of pasta, rice, potatoes and millet with poultry and meat dishes, or add it to hot winter soups.

225g (8oz) barley
1·2 litres (2pt) boiling water
1½ tsp salt

1 Put all ingredients into a saucepan and bring to boil, stirring.

2 Lower heat and cover. Simmer gently for 50 minutes, stirring from time to time, and topping up with extra water if barley seems to be drying out.

MILLET WITH ONIONS

Serves 4 to 6

Strictly NOT for the birds, this side attraction can happily replace rice or bulgar and the dried onions, added for flavour, brown on their own (a brainwave) without additional fat or oil.

225g (8oz) millet
2 tblsp dried onions, generous measure
750ml (1¼pt) boiling water
1 level tsp salt

134

1 Tip millet into saucepan with onion flakes and heat until just beginning to turn golden brown. Stir often to prevent burning.

2 Pour in boiling water and salt, lower heat, cover and simmer for 20 minutes.

3 Drain if necessary, transfer to a dish and fluff up with a fork. Serve hot or cold.

VERY GREEN SALAD

Serves 4

Based on the vegetable known as Swiss chard which can be found in Greek and Cypriot food shops, this is a zesty salad in an attractive two-tone green. The chard looks a bit like pak choi or bak choi and tastes like a combination of spinach and acidy sorrel. It needs thorough washing to remove grit and the white ribs can be cut up and used as well.

1 head of Swiss chard
1 round lettuce
1 garlic clove
2 tsp walnut or hazelnut oil

1 Thoroughly wash chard and lettuce. Drain thoroughly either by shaking in a tea towel or leaving in a colander.

2 Cut both vegetables into fine strips and put into a salad bowl.

3 Peel and crush garlic, combine with oil and add to salad. Toss just before serving. Wonderful with roast poultry.

WEST AFRICAN STYLE RED BEAN AND CHICK-PEA SALAD

Serves 4 to 5

Brimming with coriander and laced with garlic, this is another of the Caribbean's cheerful exports which is easy to copy. Eat as a cold main course with chicken and freshly cooked white rice.

1 can (439g or 15½oz) red kidney beans, drained
1 can (439g or 15½oz) chick-peas, drained
15g (½oz) fresh coriander
1 garlic clove, peeled and crushed
1 tsp oil
2 tsp lemon juice

1 Tip beans and peas into a mixing bowl.

2 Finely chop coriander and add to bowl with garlic.

3 Beat together oil and lemon juice.

4 Add to beans and peas then toss well together to mix. Cover and refrigerate lightly. Transfer to a salad bowl to serve.

TUNISIAN MECHOUIA SALAD

Serves 8

A salad which appears all over the Med and North Africa, it is also known as Meshwiya and belongs to summer when all the vegetables are ripe and brilliantly coloured. The capers add their own brand of piquancy.

1 medium sized EACH: green, yellow and red pepper
boiling water
450 to 500g (1lb) tomatoes, blanched and skinned
225g (8oz) mild salad onions
1 tblsp drained capers
4 tblsp fresh lemon juice
1 tsp salt
oil

1 Halve and de-seed peppers. Put into a saucepan, cover with water and bring back to boil. Cover and simmer for 5 minutes.

2 Drain and rinse under cold water. Squeeze dry in a clean tea towel then chop fairly finely. Put into a mixing bowl.

3 Chop tomatoes and onions. Add to peppers with capers, lemon juice and salt.

4 Toss well to mix then transfer to 8 salad plates. Trickle a little oil over each.

SPECIAL SLAW WITH SUNFLOWER SEEDS AND DEVIL DRESSING

Serves 8 to 10

The ever popular slaw, this one for parties, perked up with a spicy dressing and enriched with healthy sunflower seeds.

1kg (2lb) white cabbage
225g (8oz) carrots
225g (8oz) celery
50g (2oz) sunflower seeds, toasted under the grill
3 tblsp tomato ketchup
2 tblsp lemon juice
2 tblsp Worcestershire sauce
2 tsp coarse grained mustard
1 tblsp oil
3 to 4 shakes Tabasco

1 Finely shred cabbage and carrot and put into a large mixing bowl.

2 Cut celery into very thin diagonal strips and add to bowl with the sunflower seeds.

3 Beat together remaining ingredients. Add to slaw and toss well to mix.

4 Cover and store in the refrigerator until ready to serve. Toss again.

RAITA

A cooling and refreshing Indian side dish to team with tandooris and curries.

250g (8oz) set yogurt
1 medium tomato
2 spring onions, trimmed
¼ tsp bottled mint in vinegar or 2 tsp finely chopped fresh mint
¼ tsp salt

1 Tip yogurt into a bowl.

2 Chop tomatoes coarsely. Repeat with spring onions.

3 Add both to yogurt with mint and salt.

4 Mix thoroughly and spoon into a dish for serving.

SAVOURY PANCAKES

Make as Pancakes for Anytime (page 178) but omit sugar and substitute any savoury flavoured salt for the mixed spice. Also add 2 tsp poppy or sesame seeds. Fill with:

flaked tuna and thin onion rings
mashed pilchards in tomato sauce mixed with both chopped chives and parsley
chopped smoked salmon trimmings mixed with finely grated lemon peel then folded into fromage frais
chopped cooked chicken in Basic White Sauce (page 146) with cooked sweetcorn and a little chopped fresh ginger

CARAWAY CABBAGE

Serves 4 to 6

With origins in Norway, this is a tempered down version of what tastes a bit like hot sauerkraut without the sharpness. It has plenty of character and is an out-of-the-ordinary way of cooking cabbage.

675g (1½lb) firm white cabbage
4 tblsp water
3 tblsp cider or white wine vinegar
25g (1oz) soft brown sugar
2 level tsp caraway seeds

1 Finely shred cabbage and transfer to a large saucepan with all remaining ingredients.

2 Bring to boil, stirring all the time, cover pan and lower heat. Simmer slowly for 1½ hours, stirring occasionally, until cabbage becomes deep cream in colour with a hint of gold.

3 Cool, keep covered and refrigerate overnight for flavours to mature. Reheat gently before serving and eat very hot.

*B*RAISED CHICORY WITH LEMON

Serves 6

Rated in the UK less than in Europe, chicory is mild and delicate when cooked, reminiscent of asparagus. It makes an enterprising accompaniment to chicken and fish dishes and can also be served as a side dish with Chinese stir-frys.

6 medium sized heads of chicory
150ml (¼pt) vegetable stock (use cube and water in the absence of the real thing)
1 garlic clove, peeled and crushed
1 tblsp lemon juice

1 Set oven to 190°C (375°F), Gas 5.

2 Trim chicory and halve lengthwise. Place in an oblong dish, cut sides down.

3 Mix stock with garlic and lemon juice. Spoon over chicory then cover dish with matching lid or foil. Cook 35 minutes. Uncover and serve hot or cold.

SAUCES
AND
DRESSINGS

ONION AND WHISKY SAUCE

Serves about 6

A safe bet for any cooked meat, hot or cold, and adapted from a recipe I came across in Montreal.

450 to 500g (1lb) onions
600ml (1pt) water
1 to 1½ tsp salt
¼ tsp ground nutmeg
2 tblsp cornflour
4 tblsp whisky

1 Peel and very thinly slice onions then put into a saucepan with the water and salt.

2 Bring to boil, lower heat and cover. Simmer gently for 30 minutes or until onions are soft. Add nutmeg.

3 Blend cornflour smoothly with whisky. Add to onions and heat gently, stirring, until sauce comes to the boil and thickens.

4 Simmer 3 minutes before serving.

COCKTAIL DRESSING

Makes about 300ml (¹/₂pt)

An all-purpose effort for using both as a salad dressing and with fish and poultry cocktails.

225g (8oz) set yogurt
2 tsp Worcestershire sauce
1 tsp lemon juice
1 tsp creamed horseradish
2 tblsp tomato ketchup
1 tblsp tomato purée
5 drops Tabasco

1 Tip yogurt into a bowl, add all remaining ingredients and whisk lightly until smoothly and evenly combined.

2 Cover and refrigerate up to 4 days.

LIGHT SALAD DRESSING

Makes just over 300ml (¹/₂pt)

I recalled this from my dimming distant past when I was involved with experimental recipe work using evaporated milk for people on special diets. It's a low fat dressing – even lower now that evaporated milk is partly skimmed – and converts into an all-purpose sauce for a variety of salads. Handy.

1 carton (215g or 7½ fluid oz) Carnation 'light' evaporated milk
3 tblsp malt vinegar
¹/₂ tsp salt
1 tsp prepared English mustard
125g (4oz) fromage frais

1 Pour milk into a bowl.

2 Beat in vinegar, salt, mustard and fromage frais.

3 Cover and refrigerate up to 3 days.

BASIC WHITE SAUCE

Serves 4

A light sauce, almost completely fatless, which is useful to moisten all manner of foods from chicken to fish to vegetables. It takes just a few minutes to make, doesn't go lumpy and takes well to additions.

1½ tblsp cornflour
300ml (½pt) milk
½ tsp salt

1 Tip cornflour into a saucepan. Mix smoothly with a little milk then work in remainder.

2 Bring to boil, stirring continuously. Simmer 1 minute and season with salt. Use hot.

VARIATIONS

Add:
2 to 3 tblsp finely chopped parsley or chives
2 tsp prepared English mustard and 1 tsp vinegar
50g (2oz) thinly sliced mushrooms BEFORE bringing to the boil
75g (3oz) boiled and chopped onion with ¼ tsp nutmeg
1 slightly rounded tblsp white or soft brown sugar for a sweet sauce to go with puddings

DESSERTS
AND
CAKES

GINGER PUDDING WITH HONEYED APPLE SAUCE

Serves 4 to 6

I discovered the pudding, actually called a cake, in a small World War 2 recipe book which accounts for the absence of egg. It's a cheerful, squashy sweet for winter and a gem with its own matching apple sauce. Filling too. I've changed things round a bit and substituted brown flour for white and skimmed milk for full cream and it doesn't seem to have made a jot of difference. Because of the amount of margarine, keep this for when you can afford to be indulgent or think you deserve special treatment!

350g (12oz) wholemeal self-raising flour
1 tsp bicarbonate of soda
3 tsp ginger
½ tsp mixed spice
50g (2oz) margarine
175g (6oz) light brown sugar
2 tblsp golden syrup
300ml (½pt) skimmed milk

1 Brush a 1·2 litre (2pt) pie dish lightly with margarine. Set oven to 160°C (325°F), Gas 3.

2 Tip flour into mixing bowl. Sift in next 3 ingredients.

3 Rub in margarine finely, mix in sugar then add syrup and milk.

4 Using a fork, stir ingredients briskly together until evenly combined.

5 Spread smoothly into prepared dish and bake for 45 minutes. Spoon out of dish on to warm plates and top with hot apple sauce (Page 151).

HONEYED APPLE SAUCE

Serves 4 to 6

750g (1½lb) cooking apples
150ml (¼pt) hot water
2 cloves
5 tblsp honey

1 Peel, core and slice apples. Transfer to pan then add water and cloves.

2 Bring to boil, cover and cook over a medium heat for 5 to 7 minutes.

3 Leave in pan and beat with wooden spoon or spatula until apples soften and become pulpy. Remove cloves.

4 Stir in honey and reheat until hot before serving.

HARVEST PUDDING

Each pudding serves 8 to 10

An old-fashioned, warm-hearted pudding which is a stunner served with custard powder custard made with skimmed milk, lightly sweetened and flavoured with 1 tsp finely grated lemon peel.

Make as Fruit and Nut Cake (page 188), turn out of tins and serve one cake hot, cut into thickish slices. The other can be kept in the refrigerator or deep frozen. The microwave can be used for defrosting and also warming up cold cake.

FIGGY PUDDING

Serves 8

A heart-warming memory of childhood – heavenly with a drizzle of custard or the simple fruit sauce which follows. I microwaved mine for 4½ minutes in a 650 watt but it can also be steamed conventionally for 1½ to 2 hours.

175g (6oz) plain malted brown flour (granary)
175g (6oz) plain white flour
4 tsp baking powder
½ tsp bicarbonate of soda
2 tsp mixed spice
50g (2oz) margarine
150g (5oz) dried figs
50g (2oz) light muscovado sugar
75g (3oz) black treacle
300ml (½pt) milk

SAUCE
2 cans (each 411g or 14½oz) pears in natural juice

1 Brush a 1·25 litre (2½pt) glass basin lightly with melted margarine.

2 Tip malted flour into a mixing bowl. Sift in white flour, baking powder, bicarbonate of soda and spice. Rub in margarine.

3 Snip figs into small pieces then toss into dry ingredients with the sugar.

4 Mix to a soft consistency with the treacle and milk, stirring briskly without beating.

5 Transfer to prepared basin and cover with cling film for microwaving or foil if to be steamed conventionally.

6 Snip film twice to allow steam to escape. Microwave for 4 minutes at full power in 650 watt microwave.

7 Invert on to a plate without removing basin. Microwave a further ¾ minute.

8 Turn out on to a warm plate, remove basin and spoon portions into dishes.

9 To make sauce, tip fruit and liquid from cans into a blender goblet or food processor and run machine until smooth.

SPICED SWEET POTATOES

Serves 2

A perfect sweet for the microwave which requires the minimum of preparation.

1 by 450 to 400g (1lb) sweet potato with pinkish skin
a little brown sugar or golden syrup
sprinkle of cinnamon

1 Wash potato, prick skin with a fork then cut in half lengthwise.

2 Put on to a plate, cover with kitchen paper and cook for 8 to 9 minutes on full power in 650 watt microwave oven. When ready, the potato halves should feel tender when pressed between fingers.

3 Stand for 3 minutes. Mash flesh in their skins then top with sugar or syrup and a sprinkling of cinnamon. Eat hot.

BREAD PUDDING WITH BRANDIED MANGO SAUCE

Serves 6 to 8

Star class and quite the most welcoming pudding in the book. It belonged to my grandmother who, in the absence of mangoes (she'd never even seen one) served it always with stewed apples laced with cloves and golden syrup.

450 to 500g (1lb) fresh brown bread
boiling water
125g (4oz) raisins
3 tsp mixed spice
25g (1oz) margarine, melted
6 rounded tblsp raspberry jam
2 tblsp golden granulated sugar

1 Set oven to 180°C (350°F), Gas 4. Lightly oil a heatproof dish or small tin about 20 by 15 by 4cm in depth (8 by 6 by 1½ inches).

2 Break bread into pieces, put into a large bowl and cover with boiling water. Soak about 1 minute then drain and leave until cool enough to handle.

3 Add raisins, spice, margarine and jam. Beat well together until evenly combined.

4 Spread smoothly into prepared dish or tin and sprinkle with the sugar.

5 Bake 30 minutes. Reduce temperature to 160°C (325°F), Gas 3 and continue to bake a further hour.

6 Cut into portions and serve hot with cold mango sauce (Page 155).

BRANDIED MANGO SAUCE

Serves 6 to 8

A super sauce for spooning over hot puddings and sorbets, or rippling into fromage frais to give you an original sweet without effort.

1 can (425g or 15oz) mangoes in syrup
2 tblsp brandy

1 Whizz mangoes, syrup and brandy to a smooth purée in a blender goblet.

2 Spoon into a jug and serve cold.

EXOTIC FRUIT SALAD WITH MELON LIQUEUR

Serves 8 to 10

A party piece, and a must for winter to bring a touch of brightness and lightness to life. Serve plain or top each serving with fromage frais.

9 nectarines
2 Galia or Ogen melons
6 Sharon fruit
5 tblsp Midori (melon liqueur from Japan) or any other fruity liqueur, depending on preference

1 Wash nectarines, halve and remove stones. Cut unpeeled flesh into thin wedges and transfer to a large mixing bowl.

2 Halve and de-seed melons then scoop flesh into bowl with a teaspoon or melon baller.

3 Wash and dry Sharon fruit. Coarsely chop and add to the other fruits with liqueur. Toss over and over with a spoon to mix.

4 Cover with a plate and refrigerate for at least 2 hours.

TIP

Midori liqueur is bright green and easily recognisable.

FROMAGE FRAIS FIG DESSERT WITH GINGER AND ORANGE

Serves 4

A lazy cook's dessert, fabulous chilled in hot weather and a bit off the beaten track.

500g (1lb) fromage frais
1 can (425g or 15oz) figs in syrup, drained
2 tblsp fig syrup from can
4 knobs preserved ginger in syrup
2 tsp grated orange peel

1 Transfer fromage frais to a bowl.

2 Cut up figs and stir in with fig syrup.

3 Thinly slice ginger. Add to mixture and fold in with a spoon.

4 Arrange in 4 dishes, refrigerate until well-chilled and sprinkle orange peel over the top of each before serving.

COFFEE YOGURT WITH BROWN SUGAR

Serves 4

A simple yet sophisticated sweet.

500g (1lb) set yogurt
3 tsp instant coffee
1 tblsp hot water
125g (4oz) demerara sugar

1 Spoon yogurt into a bowl.

2 Dissolve coffee in the water. Stir into yogurt with sugar.

3 Transfer to dessert dishes and eat straight away before the sugar has time to melt – the crunchiness is the best part.

SHARON FRUIT CUPS WITH COTTAGE CHEESE AND RAISIN HEARTS

Serves 6

Sweet, juicy and totally hassle-free, make in winter when Israeli Sharons are in full swing. Avoid persimmons, their close relations, as they are too soft to hold their shape.

6 medium to large Sharon fruit
175g (6oz) cottage cheese
25g (1oz) raisins
6 clementine segments
6 leaves from a round lettuce, washed and gently dried

1 Wash and dry Sharon fruit then cut tops off each, just as you would if you were making stuffed tomatoes. Keep lids aside for time being.

2 With a grapefruit knife, carefully cut out flesh of Sharons, taking every care not to pierce the skins.

3 Chop flesh coarsely. Combine with cottage cheese and raisins then spoon into Sharon cups.

4 Transfer to a plate, top with lids and refrigerate several hours to firm up.

5 Before serving, decorate each with a clementine segment and stand on a flatish dish lined with lettuce.

WINTER FRUIT BRÛLÉE WITH FROMAGE FRAIS

Serves 4 to 6

Great expectations for this one and it certainly comes up to scratch. You can keep it up your sleeve for Christmas when Israeli Sharon fruits (tomato look-alikes) and fresh dates begin to emerge. Or make it on and off until early spring before both fruits bow out of our lives until next year.

8 Sharon fruit
225g (8oz) fresh dates
500g (1lb) fromage frais
175g (6oz) golden granulated sugar

1 Cut Sharon fruits into wedges as you would tomatoes. Put into mixing bowl.

2 Skin dates, halve and remove stones. Add to Sharons with fromage frais.

3 Toss gently to mix, transfer to a heatproof dish (not too deep) then sprinkle top with sugar.

4 Place under a hot grill until sugar caramelises.

5 Refrigerate until well chilled before serving.

JELLIED RASPBERRY 'CREAMS'

Serves 4

Light, short-cut little puddings with the fragrance of summer fruits.

1 blackcurrant flavour jelly
boiling water
2 tblsp cornflour
300ml (½pt) cold milk
1 tsp vanilla essence
350g (12oz) raspberries, stalks removed, rinsed, drained or use frozen if more
convenient

1 Break jelly cubes into a saucepan, mix in boiling water and melt over a low heat, stirring continuously. Keep aside temporarily.

2 Tip cornflour into saucepan and blend smoothly with a little cold milk. Pour in remainder and cook, stirring all the time, until sauce comes to the boil and thickens. Simmer 2 minutes.

3 Gently whisk in liquid jelly and vanilla, then carefully fork in raspberries, taking care not to break them up too much. Note that frozen raspberries need only be partially thawed.

4 Transfer to 4 dishes and refrigerate until well chilled.

ORANGE COCKTAILS WITH SOFT FRUIT SAUCE

Serves 4

A fruity creation, elegant with a deep red sauce.

1 orange flavour jelly
300ml (½pt) boiling water
350g (12oz) fromage frais

1 Break jelly cubes into a saucepan, mix in boiling water and melt over a low heat, stirring continuously.

2 Cool to lukewarm then refrigerate until cold but still liquid.

3 Whisk gradually into the fromage frais, divide equally between 4 stemmed glasses and chill until firm.

4 Before serving, float a layer of fruit sauce on top of each (Page 163).

FRUIT SAUCE

Serves 6 to 8

One of our favourites at any time of year and no problem now with berry fruits so readily available at freezer centres.

450 to 500g (1lb) mixed berry fruits such as raspberries, strawberries and blackcurrants (or choice of only one or two fruits as required)
1 level tsp cornflour
50g (2oz) icing sugar, sifted
5 tblsp cold water

1 If using fresh fruits, rinse and remove stalks. This is not necessary with frozen fruits. Tip into a saucepan.

2 Warm through, stirring, as this somehow brings out the flavours.

3 Transfer to a blender goblet or food processor and whizz to a purée.

4 Rub through a fine mesh sieve directly into a bowl to eliminate seeds.

5 Return liquid to saucepan and add cornflour, sugar and water, all blended smoothly together.

6 Bring to the boil, stirring all the time, and simmer for 1 minute when sauce should thicken slightly and look clear and glossy. Serve cold.

VANILLA WHIP WITH STRAWBERRY

A light-hearted sweet which should suit the whole family.

1 packet vanilla blancmange
600ml (1pt) cold milk
5 tblsp fruity strawberry jam
2 egg whites from Grade 3 eggs
pinch of salt
small fresh strawberries or fresh cherries to decorate

1 Make up blancmange with milk as directed on the packet.

2 Once thickened, stir in the jam.

3 Beat egg whites to a thick, stiff snow with salt.

4 Gently whisk into the blancmange. When smooth and evenly-combined, transfer to 4 dishes and chill thoroughly in the refrigerator.

5 Decorate with fresh fruit immediately before serving.

EASTERN RICE PUDDING WITH ROSE AND CARDAMOM

Serves 4

A temptress from the East to enjoy at the end of any Oriental meal.

600ml (1pt) milk
50g (2oz) flaked rice
4 tblsp caster sugar
seeds from 3 opened out cardamom pods
1 tblsp rose water, available from some pharmacies to order
silver dragees

1 Pour milk into saucepan. Add rice and slowly bring to the boil, stirring continuously.

2 Simmer 3 minutes or until well thickened. Mix in sugar, cardamom seeds and rose water.

3 Transfer to 4 dishes. Cool, then cover and refrigerate until well chilled.

4 Sprinkle each portion sparingly with the dragees before serving.

ON THE SPOT CHERRY MOUSSE

Serves 4

You can come in at any time of day or night and make a breezy, fast sweet in next to no time. This one has a dash of kirsch to set the taste buds tingling.

1 can (400g or 14oz) cherry fruit pie filling
1 tblsp kirsch
3 egg whites from Grade 3 eggs
pinch of salt

1 Spoon fruit pie filling into a saucepan and bring gently to the boil, stirring all the time.

2 Mix in kirsch and leave pan over low heat.

3 Whisk egg whites stiffly with salt, then, using a metal spoon, fold smoothly and evenly into hot fruit mixture.

4 Transfer to 4 dishes or glasses and refrigerate 2 to 3 hours until well chilled.

5 Make and eat on same day as mixture tends to separate out on standing.

PEARS IN CIDER WITH CLOVES AND CINNAMON

Serves 8

An elegant contribution to the 'sweet trolley', made in the microwave for relative speed. Well-suited to entertaining.

450ml (¾pt) sweet cider
75g (3oz) soft brown sugar
1 cinnamon stick
2 cloves
8 medium dessert pears with stalks
2 level tblsp cornflour
5 tblsp cold water
1 tsp vanilla essence
½ tsp finely grated orange peel

1 Pour cider into a dish of 2·75 litre (5pt) capacity and about 10cm (4 inches) deep. Add sugar, cinnamon stick and cloves. Leave uncovered and cook for 3 minutes at full power in a 650 watt microwave.

2 Peel pears carefully without removing stalks. Stand upright in a dish then cover with a plate.

3 Cook 4 minutes. Baste pears with liquid in dish, cover as before and cook 6 minutes. Remove pears to serving dish.

4 Mix cornflour smoothly with water, essence and orange peel. Add to liquid in dish, leave uncovered and cook 5 minutes until thickened, stirring 3 times.

5 Pour over pears. Cover and refrigerate when cold. Serve well chilled.

6 Red grape juice may be used instead of cider.

MINTED LEMON MERINGUE PUDDINGS

Serves 4

Adapted from Florida's Key Lime Pie, you can't go wrong with this semi-instant sweet, topped with a cloud of uncooked meringue. A word of warning though – make it and eat quickly as the meringue begins to weep and sag if it's left to stand for too long.

1 can (405g or 14·3oz) skimmed and sweetened condensed milk
juice and finely grated peel of 2 medium lemons
½ tsp very finely chopped mint
1 egg white from Grade 3 egg
40g (1½oz) caster sugar

1 Tip condensed milk into a bowl and stir in lemon juice, lemon peel and mint.

2 Divide between 4 dishes and refrigerate 2 to 3 hours or until set.

3 Before serving, whisk egg white to a stiff snow then gradually beat in the sugar.

4 When meringue stands in firm peaks, spoon on top of the puddings.

SUMMER PUDDING

Serves 8

Marvellous as ever, guaranteed to tantalise eyes and taste-buds, typically English. I use more bread than most other food writers but for me, at any rate, the pudding works better and, inevitably, goes further. It's perfection on its own but for those accustomed to swishing cream over their helpings, I suggest they switch to fromage frais or yogurt instead.

1kg (2lb) mixed berry fruits, fresh or frozen
125g (4oz) light brown soft sugar
10 slices soft grain bread with oats (smallish slices)

1 Prepare fruit according to type if fresh. Rinse in a colander then transfer to a saucepan. Alternatively put frozen fruits directly into pan and leave over a low heat until half de-frosted.

2 Add sugar and leave over a low heat until juices run. Simmer gently for about 4 to 5 minutes. Cool to lukewarm.

3 Decrust bread and cut each slice in half lengthwise. Use 3 to 4 slices to line base and sides of an ungreased 1·5 litre (2½pt) pudding basin. Make sure there are no gaps anywhere.

4 Fill with alternate layers of bread, fruit and juice. Do this slowly to ensure bread becomes saturated from bottom of basin to top. Finish with a layer of bread.

5 Top with a fitting plate which sits directly on top of pudding and weigh down with something heavy – a brick or garden stones.

6 Keep leftover juice (there will be some spare) covered in the refrigerator.

7 Refrigerate pudding for 12 to 24 hours. Turn out into a shallow dish to catch the juices which inevitably seep out of the bread.

8 Coat with leftover juice and spoon pudding on to plates.

MANGO KULFI

Serves 6

A short-cut version of mine for a traditional Indian ice cream which is the easiest thing in the world to make.

2 medium ripe mangoes or 1 can (425g or 15oz) mangoes in syrup
1 can (400g or 14oz) skimmed and sweetened condensed milk
seeds from 3 opened out green cardamom pods

1 Peel mangoes, cut flesh away from centre stone and put into a blender or food processor. Alternatively, tip in canned mangoes and their syrup and blend either to a smooth purée.

2 Scrape into a bowl and whisk in milk and cardamom seeds. Cover and freeze for about 2 hours.

3 Re-whisk gently, cover again and freeze several hours until firm. Scoop into small dishes for serving.

MACARONI MILK PUDDING WITH ABUNDANT FRUITS

Serves 4

Shades of schooldays but a little more adult.

600ml (1pt) milk
150g (5oz) quick cooking macaroni
50g (2oz) molasses sugar (very dark and treacly)
50g (2oz) raisins
50g (2oz) glacé pineapple
50g (2oz) glacé cherries
50g (2oz) crystallised ginger (sugar-coated)
50g (2oz) walnuts
½ tsp mixed spice
15g (½oz) margarine, melted

1 Set oven to 150°C (300°F), Gas 3.

2 Pour milk into a pan and add the macaroni, sugar and raisins.

3 Chop pineapple, cherries and ginger into fairly coarse pieces. Add to pan.

4 Bring to the boil, leave uncovered and simmer gently for 10 minutes.

5 Meanwhile chop nuts and add to pudding with spice.

6 Spoon into a 900ml (1½pt) lightly greased heatproof dish and trickle margarine over the top.

7 Bake for 40 minutes and serve hot.

PINEAPPLE RICE PUDDING WITH WALNUTS

Serves 4

One up on a nursery milk pudding and rapidly made in the microwave.

1 can (440g/about 14½oz) low fat rice pudding
1 can (432g or 15½oz) 8 unsweetened pineapple slices in natural juice
3 heaped tblsp apricot or pineapple jam
50g (2oz) chopped walnuts

1 Spread rice pudding into a 20cm (8 inch) round dish.

2 Drain pineapple, reserving juice. Arrange fruit on top of rice.

3 Pour juice into a pan and add the jam. Bring slowly to the boil, stirring, and bubble until thick – about 7 minutes.

4 Sprinkle walnuts over pudding then coat with pineapple syrup.

5 Cover with cling film, nick twice and reheat for 4 minutes at full power in a 650 watt microwave.

LEMON FROST

Serves 8

A chilly finish and somewhat akin to Italy's granita – flavoured ice crystals which melt on the tongue like snowflakes.

1 litre (1¾pt) freshly squeezed lemonade or old fashioned lemonade, opened and left
to lose its fizz
2 egg whites from Grade 3 eggs
pinch of salt

1 Pour lemonade into a bowl then cover and freeze until almost hard.

2 Whip egg whites and salt together until stiff.

3 Break up lemonade until it looks grainy then fold in whites.

4 Cover and freeze until hard. Before serving, soften down a little then quickly scrape portions into bowls. Serve immediately as it melts fast.

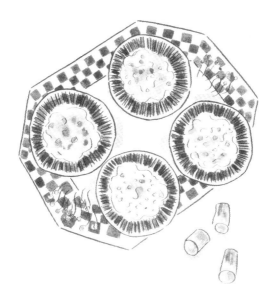

VANILLA JELLY "MOUSSE"

Serves 6

Low fat, low cholesterol, low sugar – what more could one ask. Silken in texture and resembling jelly, blancmange, junket and thick cream all rolled into one, use this for filling big or little meringues; for spooning over fresh, stewed or canned fruit; as a fast dessert in individual dishes with toppings of jam, honey or syrup, liquid coffee essence such as Camp or fruit liqueurs.

150ml (¼pt) cold water
1 envelope gelatine
2 tblsp caster sugar
225 to 250g (8oz) fromage frais
225 to 250g (8oz) set yogurt
1 tsp vanilla essence

1 Pour cold water into a saucepan. Add gelatine and sugar then stand over low heat until crystals dissolve and liquid is clear.

2 Cool to lukewarm. Spoon last three ingredients into a bowl then gently beat in the gelatine mixture.

3 Refrigerate until thickened and only just beginning to set (watch carefully or it might set too firmly).

4 Whip until fluffy and aerated, cover and refrigerate until firm. For individual puddings, set in dishes or bowls.

SKYR ICE CREAM WITH FRUIT

Serves about 10

I've chosen strawberries, because I love them so much, for this particular ice cream but raspberries, blackberries, loganberries or imported blueberries would do just as well. Though not as smooth or as creamy as commercial varieties of low fat ice cream because I don't have the technical know-how, it is a passable imitation and, scooped into cornets, is instant goodness for children without being over-sweet or fatty. I've noticed adults are partial to it as well but please do remember it's a bit crystally. I don't want you disappointed.

Icelandic Skyr (page 176) made with 450 to 500g (1lb) EACH: fromage frais and set yogurt
150g (5oz) honey or golden syrup
1 envelope gelatine
100ml (3½ fluid oz) cold water
225g (8oz) sliced strawberries
3 tblsp raspberry jam

1 Combine fromage frais and yogurt together in a fairly large mixing bowl.

2 Put honey or syrup, gelatine and water into a small saucepan and leave over a low heat until gelatine has melted and liquid is clear. Stir from time to time.

3 Beat into the yogurt and fromage frais. Cover and freeze until 2·5cm (1 inch) of mixture has solidified and hardened round edge of bowl.

4 Beat until light and frothy. Slice strawberries and warm through in a small pan with the jam.

5 Fold into the Skyr, cover and freeze until firm. Allow to soften a little at kitchen temperature before scooping or spooning out.

ICELANDIC SKYR

Pronounced skier and as much part of the Icelandic way of life as beans and toast are over here, this low-fat dairy product has many uses and makes a superior, almost no-fat substitute for cream. Try it spooned into bowls and sprinkled with crunchy demerara sugar for a fast sweet. Serve with breakfast cereals and over canned and fresh fruit. Convert into ice cream. Season with salt and pepper and use as a savoury salad dressing. To make, simply mix together equal parts of set yogurt and fromage frais. Cover and refrigerate until needed.

THE ALTERNATIVE CHEESE CAKE

Serves 12

A marvellous contribution, sumptuous and seemingly rich, made from medium fat soft cheese and versatile tofu. Good old British custard powder gives the cake a warm golden colour one associates with eggs and I consider this a personal triumph of a low fat recipe. Keep it for grand occasions, parties, buffets and summer tea in the garden and I bet you no-one will know if it's the real thing or not. Have a go and remember to top the cake with brightly coloured fruits; strawberries, kiwis, starfruits, cherries or even canned fruit fillings.

75g (3oz) bran flakes, crushed
350g (12oz) medium fat soft cheese
342g (about 12oz) tofu, drained
175g (6oz) golden granulated sugar
40g (1½oz) custard powder

1 tsp vanilla essence
5 Grade 1 or 2 egg whites
strained juice of 1 medium lemon

1 Lightly grease a 23cm (9 inch) spring clip tin. Set oven to 150°C (300°F), Gas 3.

2 Press crushed bran flakes over base of tin. Spoon cheese into a food processor. Break up tofu and add with the sugar, custard, essence, egg whites and lemon juice.

3 Blend until smooth then gently and lightly ladle into tin. If you hurry this process, the flakes might rise up into the cheese mixture.

4 Cook 1 hour 10 minutes, open the oven door then leave cake where it is until lukewarm.

5 Remove from oven. When completely cold, unclip sides and carefully lift off.

6 Refrigerate cheese cake for several hours before serving, then decorate with fruit.

PANCAKES FOR ANYTIME

Makes 8

Soft, velvety and made without egg yolks, these are highly recommended rolled up with fillings or soaked in perfumed syrup, a custom from the Middle East. Suggestions follow.

225g (8oz) self-raising flour
1 tsp mixed spice (optional)
2 tblsp caster sugar
2 tsp oil
300ml (½pt) milk
2 egg whites from Grade 1 or 2 eggs
pinch of salt
1 tblsp sparkling mineral water

1 Sift flour and spice if used into a bowl. Toss in sugar.

2 Add oil then gradually beat in milk. Continue to beat until mixture is smooth – you'll find consistency on the thick side.

3 Beat egg whites to a stiff snow with the salt. Gently whisk into batter mixture with mineral water.

4 Heat a 20cm (8 inch) non-stick pan until hot. Spread in enough batter to cover base smoothly – not too thick.

5 When underside is golden, flip over and fry second side until brown speckles appear.

6 To keep warm, stack on to a plate standing over a pan of gently boiling water and cover with lid until ready to serve as suggested below:

PANCAKES WITH MARMALADE AND BANANA

Spread each pancake with chunky orange marmalade. Top with 3 sliced bananas which is enough for all the pancakes then roll up and serve.

PANCAKES WITH APPLE

Fill each pancake with hot apple purée. Roll up and serve.

PANCAKES WITH COTTAGE CHEESE AND FRUIT

Fill each pancake with cottage cheese mixed with either chopped dried dates or peeled and coarsely chopped dessert pears.

SYRUP DRENCHED PANCAKES

Serves 8

Too good to be true!

8 Pancakes for Anytime (page 178)
225g (8oz) caster sugar
150ml (¼pt) water
1 tblsp lemon juice
2 tblsp peach or apricot brandy
1 tblsp orange flower water, available from some pharmacies to order
fromage frais

1 Keep pancakes hot on a plate resting over a pan of simmering water.

2 For syrup, tip sugar into a saucepan. Add water and heat gently until sugar dissolves. Bring to boil and bubble for 5 minutes.

3 Stir in lemon juice, peach or apricot brandy and the orange flower water.

4 Transfer stack of pancakes to a shallow dish.

5 Coat with hot syrup which should then penetrate each one. Refrigerate until cold and, before serving, cut into eight wedges like a cake.

6 Serve pancake wedges topped with tablespoons of fromage frais.

BIRCHER-BENNER BREAKFAST MUESLI

Serves 4

A genuine enough article, based on the original recipe created by Dr Bircher-Benner who won fame and acclaim for his nature cure clinic in Zurich, Switzerland. It's worth a go for breakfast or dessert from time to time when seasonal fruits can be added according to whim – soft summer fruits are heaven. What delights me is that one food manufacturer, Fussell's, have had the nous to make sweetened condensed milk (a must for this recipe) from skimmed milk, thus reducing fat and making the Muesli viable for people watching their cholesterol intake and also weight.

12 tblsp porridge oats
3 tblsp oat bran (my addition)
600ml (1pt) cold water
6 tblsp freshly squeezed lemon juice
6 well-rounded tblsp sweetened condensed milk
3 medium to large dessert apples

OPTIONAL EXTRAS
225 to 275g (8 to 10oz) seasonal soft fruits or slices of apricots, peaches, firm plums, pears

1 In fairly large bowl, combine oats, oat bran, water, lemon juice and condensed milk. Cover and refrigerate overnight.

2 If too thick for personal taste, thin down with a little extra water. Grate in unpeeled apples and mix thoroughly.

3 Spoon into cereal bowls and top each portion with fresh fruit.

CHESTNUT 'MOUSSE' WITH LIQUEUR AND RAISINS

Serves 6

A smoothie for important occasions in life. I advise small portions only as it's quite rich-tasting and also filling.

150g (5oz) raisins
6 tblsp peach, apricot or cherry brandy or cream sherry
1 can (439g or 15½oz) chestnut purée
100g (3½oz) golden caster sugar
1 tsp vanilla essence
125g (4oz) fromage frais
2 egg whites from Grade 1 or 2 eggs
pinch of salt
clusters of seedless grapes for decoration

1 Put raisins into a basin and stir in chosen alcohol. Cover and leave 8 to 10 hours at kitchen temperature.

2 Beat chestnut purée with sugar, essence and fromage frais then stir in raisins and alcohol.

3 Beat egg whites and pinch of salt to a stiff snow in a clean bowl. Fold into chestnut mixture with a metal spoon or spatula then divide between 6 stemmed glasses or small dishes.

4 Refrigerate several hours or even overnight. Decorate with grapes before serving.

UNYEASTED RAISIN 'BREAD' WITH HONEY

Makes 1 family size loaf

An easy slicer with a friendly personality and conveniently low fat. Eat with mid-morning coffee or an afternoon cup of tea. Cottage cheese and jam as a topping turns a fairly plain loaf into a glass slipper.

400g (14oz) plain wholemeal flour
1 tsp baking powder
½ tsp bicarbonate of soda
25g (1oz) margarine
225ml (8 fluid oz) clear honey, at kitchen temperature
1 Grade 3 egg, beaten
50ml (2 fluid oz) buttermilk or 25ml (1oz) skimmed milk beaten with 25g (1oz) plain yogurt
225g (8oz) raisins
175g (6oz) walnuts, chopped

1 Lightly brush a 1kg (2lb) oblong loaf tin then line base and sides with non-stick baking paper.

2 Set oven to 160°C (325°F), Gas 3. Tip flour into bowl then sift in baking powder and bicarbonate of soda.

3 In separate bowl, beat margarine and honey until smooth then gradually work in the egg. Using metal spoon, fold in dry ingredients and buttermilk or milk and yogurt mixture.

4 Stir in raisins and nuts. Spread smoothly into prepared tin and bake 2 hours until well-risen and golden brown.

5 Remove from oven, leave until lukewarm then turn out on to a wire rack.

6 Wrap in foil when completely cold and leave 1 day before cutting. Remove lining paper before serving and cut into thinnish slices. Store leftovers airtight.

ALL-WHITE 'SPONGE' CAKE

Cuts into about 8 to 9 wedges

When all said and done, a cakeless life is not exactly a bundle of laughs so I've come up with this light and well-behaved sort of a sponge which can be filled with jam and fromage frais for an approximation of the real thing. It's based on oil and contains egg whites but no yolks. Just go easy on the size of portions and eat occasionally – don't make a pig of yourself!

150g (5oz) self-raising flour
25g (1oz) cornflour
1½ tsp baking powder
pinch of salt
100ml (3½ fluid oz) light oil (NOT olive)
100ml (3½ fluid oz) water
4 egg whites from Grade 2 eggs
½ tsp vanilla essence
another pinch of salt
150g (5oz) caster sugar

1 Set oven to 190°C (375°F), Gas 5. Base-line 2 by 18cm (7 inch) non-stick sandwich tins with non-stick baking paper or greaseproof.

2 Sift first 4 dry ingredients into a bowl.

3 Whisk together oil, water, 2 egg whites and essence then beat into dry ingredients.

4 Tip remaining 2 whites into a clean, dry bowl. Add salt and beat to a stiff snow. Gradually whisk in sugar and continue whisking until mixture looks like meringue and stands in tall, shiny peaks.

5 Using a metal spoon, smoothly and evenly fold into the cake mixture.

6 Divide between tins; tap each gently to even out mixture then bake 25 minutes or until well-risen and golden.

7 Cool to lukewarm, turn out on to wire racks and remove paper when cold. Sandwich together with chosen filling just before eating. Until then, cake may be wrapped in foil and stored in the fridge for about 3 days. It should be returned to room temperature before filling.

FRUIT CLUSTERS

Makes 24

Top billing for these, designed to replace chocolate mints as after-dinner sweetmeats.

125g (4oz) each of the following dried fruits:
pears
peaches
prunes with stones already removed
hot water
125g (4oz) dried and stoned dates
12 glacé cherries, halved
12 walnut quarters

1 Soak pears, peaches and prunes for 30 minutes in hot water to cover. Drain and squeeze dry with your hands.

2 Finely chop with the dates. Draw mixture together and divide into 24 pieces.

3 Roll each into a ball and drop into paper sweet cases. Decorate half with the cherries, the balance with walnuts. Refrigerate lightly before serving.

YOGURT AND OAT BISCUITS

Makes 30

What makes you think you can't have a biscuit with your midmorning or afternoon cuppa any more. Only the pessimists. These moist little rounds, and the ones that follow, are both low fat, made with 'light' Mazola oil and this first recipe doesn't even have an egg in sight. Also no rolling out for either which has to be a bonus. All the same, no more than about 1 a day.

50ml (2 fluid oz) Mazola 'light' oil
125g (4oz) soft brown sugar
125g (4oz) yogurt
1 tsp vanilla essence
100g (3½oz) porridge oats
125g (4oz) malted brown flour (granary)
15g (½oz) wheatgerm, lightly toasted under the grill
½ tsp baking powder
1½ tsp mixed spice

1 Set oven to 190°C (375°F), Gas 5. Line 2 shallow baking trays with non-stick baking paper.

2 Pour oil into a bowl. Beat in sugar, yogurt and essence then stir in all remaining ingredients.

3 When well-combined, spoon 30 dollops, well spaced as they spread slightly, on to prepared trays. Flatten each with prongs of a fork.

4 Bake 20 to 25 minutes towards top and lower half of oven until golden brown, reversing position of trays at half time.

5 Leave on the trays until lukewarm, lift on to a wire cooling rack with a spatula and store airtight when completely cold.

ROCK CAKE COOKIES

Makes about 40

These are quite fun. A cross between a biscuit and a cake and glistening with goodness because of the egg and oil content. Eat sparingly – no more than 3 or 4 a week. In the meantime, store in an airtight container.

2 Grade 2 eggs
125ml (4 fluid oz) Mazola 'light' oil
125ml (4oz) golden syrup, melted
2 tsp cinnamon
200g (7oz) porridge oats
225g (8oz) raisins
100g (3½oz) chopped walnuts
25g (1oz) low fat milk powder
25g (1oz) oat bran

1 Set oven to 150°C (300°F), Gas 3. Line 2 shallow baking trays with non-stick baking powder.

2 Break eggs into a bowl then beat in oil, syrup and cinnamon.

3 Stir in all remaining ingredients then, with 2 spoons, arrange 20 rocky heaps on each tray.

4 Bake 25 to 30 minutes towards top and lower half of oven, reversing position of trays at half time. When ready, cookies should be light golden brown.

5 Cool almost completely then carefully transfer to a wire cooling rack. Store airtight when cold. Note that cookies tend to be crumbly.

FRUIT AND NUT CAKE

Each cuts into 12 slices

A wonderfully moist and unproblematic cake which keeps well in the fridge if well-wrapped in foil. It's a World War 2 revival and uses sparing amounts of the then scarce fat and eggs. The mixture makes two cakes so my policy is to eat one and freeze the other.

450g (1lb) wholemeal self-raising flour
1½ tsp bicarbonate of soda
2 tsp mixed spice
50g (2oz) margarine
150g (5oz) light brown soft sugar
450g (1lb) stoned dates (in a block – not rolled in sugar)
225g (8oz) dried apricots
100g (3½oz) walnuts
500ml (18 fluid oz) cold tea, tea bag removed or strained if made with tea leaves
1 Grade 1 or 2 egg, beaten

1 Set oven to 160°C (325°F), Gas 3. Lightly oil 2 by 1kg (2lb) loaf tins then line with non-stick baking paper.

2 Tip flour into a bowl then sift in soda and spice. Rub in margarine. Toss in the sugar. Leave aside for time being.

3 Chop dates. Wash apricots thoroughly, wipe dry and scissor-snip into small pieces. Chop walnuts coarsely.

4 Add both fruits and nuts to dry ingredients. Using a fork, mix to a semi-stiff mixture with the tea and egg.

5 Spread smoothly into prepared tins and bake both on one shelf in the oven for 1½ hours or until a wooden cocktail stick, inserted into the centre, comes out clean with no uncooked mixture sticking to it.

6 Cool for 30 minutes then turn out on to wire cooling racks. Foil wrap when cold and leave 1 day before cutting.

VARIATIONS
... Use fruit flavoured tea (tisane) or Earl Grey tea instead of plain
... Omit apricots for a lighter cake or use only half quantity
... Substitute dried figs for dates, stoned prunes for apricots

WALNUT PETITS FOURS

Makes about 60

I have been making walnut marzipan for a long time now, long before the experts decided walnuts had the least fat of all nuts (with chestnuts) and were acceptable for those on low cholesterol diets – within reason of course, not in great handfuls! The mixture has an absolutely superb taste, can be used instead of almond paste and makes wonderful petits fours.

BASIC MARZIPAN
300g (11oz) walnuts
75g (3oz) icing sugar
125g (4oz) light muscovado sugar
2 tsp lemon juice
1 tsp vanilla essence
1 egg white from Grade 3 egg

1 Grind walnuts in mill or blender until they are almost as fine as ground almonds. Don't over-do as nuts will get oily.

2 Spoon into a bowl, sift in icing sugar then add the muscovado sugar, lemon juice and vanilla.

3 Beat egg white until foamy. Fork into walnut mixture then knead quickly with finger tips until marzipan forms a smooth ball.

PLAIN PETITS FOURS

Break off 20 pieces of mixture and roll into even-sized marbles. Drop into paper sweet cases.

DATE AND MARZIPAN PETITS FOURS

Break off 20 pieces of mixture and pack into 20 fresh dates, skinned and stoned. Transfer to paper sweet cases and make and eat on same day.

PRUNE AND MARZIPAN PETITS FOURS

Make as above, using plump stoned prunes instead of dates.

KUMQUAT AND MARZIPAN PETITS FOURS

Pack mixture into halved and hollowed out kumquats. Make and eat on same day.

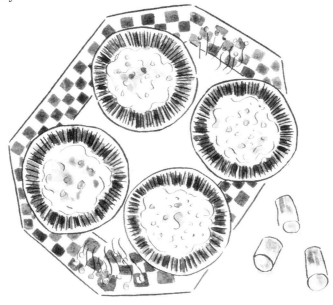

INDEX

VEGETARIAN

SALADS AND SIDE DISHES

SAUCES AND DRESSINGS

DESSERTS AND CAKES